'In *Rhythm to Recovery*, Simon Faulkner has distilled years of successful, evidence-based practice into a comprehensive series of highly accessible rhythmic exercises and reflective starting points that will be a valuable addition to any therapeutic practitioner's toolkit. What's more, he has opened up the field of rhythm work in such a way that no prior musical expertise is needed to be able to use these exercises – making this accessible to therapists, educators and group leaders who may never have considered using rhythm in their work until now. Highly recommended!'

– Dr Jane Bentley, specialist consultant,
music in health care settings

'Over the past several years Simon Faulkner has trained a large number of our school counsellors in using rhythmic based interventions. This model has been of great value for them in both individual and group work. The manual and the cards are easy to follow and very practical. My team have had great success working with children, adolescents, older people and residents in rehabilitation centres.

The versatility of the Rhythm2Recovery model makes it suitable for use with a variety of ages and presentations – from students who are very anxious and withdrawn to those that have difficulty with emotional regulation and substance abuse.

Everyone benefits from drumming – the participants are able to address issues and communicate while having fun and the facilitators enjoy it too.'

– Virgina Banks, Senior Team Leader,
School Counselling Programs, Catholic Education, Sydney

'If you are now working with, or ever planning to work with, any type of at risk population in schools, behavioural centres, hospitals, drug and alcohol rehabs, mental health rehabs, trauma services, prisons or child protection services, then you cannot afford to miss an opportunity to learn from the body of work Simon Faulkner provides in this new book.'

– Arthur Hull, Village Music Circles, CA

'The beauty of what Simon offers with the Rhythm2Recovery model is in its flexibility. I am able to tailor the program to the needs of the group. Whether in sessions with individuals all the way through to larger groups, R2R allows me the flexibility to address any number of issues that come up and for any length of time.'

– Gerard McDonnell, Senior Psychological Advisor,
Specialist Support Unit, NSW Education

RHYTHM TO RECOVERY

RHYTHM

TO

RECOVERY

A Practical Guide to Using Rhythmic
Music, Voice and Movement for
Social and Emotional Development

Simon Faulkner

Foreword by Dr James Oshinsky, PhD

Jessica Kingsley *Publishers*
London and Philadelphia

First published in 2017
by Jessica Kingsley Publishers
73 Collier Street
London N1 9BE, UK
and
400 Market Street, Suite 400
Philadelphia, PA 19106, USA

www.jkp.com

Library of Congress Cataloging in Publication Data
Names: Faulkner, Simon.
Title: Rhythm to recovery : a practical guide to using percussion, voice and
   music for social and emotional development / Simon Faulkner ; foreword by
   James Oshinsky.
Description: London ; Philadelphia : Jessica Kingsley Publishers, 2017. |
   Includes bibliographical references and index.
Identifiers: LCCN 2016022422 | ISBN 9781785921322
Subjects: LCSH: Music therapy. | Drum circles. | Socialization.
Classification: LCC ML3920 .F24 2017 | DDC 615.8/5154--dc23 LC record available at https://
urldefense.proofpoint.com/v2/url?u=https-3A__lccn.loc.gov_2016022422&d=DQIFAg&c=e
uGZstcaTDllvimEN8b7jXrwqOf-v5A_CdpgnVfiiMM&r=4EemtO9R1x-uacXap7EaQ1RHPq9-
MnYBwnfuC-ulpHU&m=g67BJCtbeF_5_OVUT4WJr09mMFIc1TWbPTBL4ContTY&s=tXM_
piF1S7-Sj59R7amJtTxB6qUtqVheSRSXQa-FZes&e=

British Library Cataloguing in Publication Data
A CIP catalogue record for this book is available from the British Library

ISBN 978 1 78592 132 2
eISBN 978 1 78450 397 0

Printed and bound in Great Britain

The accompanying materials can be found at www.jkp.com/voucher using the code RHYTHM2RECOVERY

CONTENTS

FOREWORD

When Simon Faulkner asked me to write a foreword for his book on the use of drumming and other forms of rhythmic music and movement for promoting social-emotional learning, I was flattered and excited. He and I belong to a somewhat small fraternity of dual-credentialed folk who are both professional therapists/counsellors and at least amateur musicians, operating outside the boundaries of traditional clinical music therapy. We have seen first hand the powerful and transformative influences of group music making on populations that historically have been considered hard to reach. We have put in the time trying out variations on talk-based groups and education-based programs, and we know both the value and the limitations of these approaches.

Therapists and educators have always known that lived experience is a more powerful teaching method for social skills than even the best word-based lessons. It is not hard to create lessons that contain pro-social content. But clients low in social awareness or motivation can act 'as if' they had internalised empathy or assertiveness that have not truly rooted. Our personal stories, when told in words, require exposure that overtaxes modest levels of group trust. So clients, out of self-preservation, risk less or conform superficially. This does not lead to healing or lasting change.

What has been needed is a method that provides vivid experiences through which clients can feel their place in a group, experiment with social limits in a safe manner and take risks to discover their personal identity. Drumming and other forms of rhythmic exercises are effective as mediums for social interaction and growth because they are first and foremost inherently enjoyable, and because the level of coordinated listening, observing and responding is immediately apparent. The feedback loop between participation and evaluation is immediate, visceral and wordless. This is powerful 'body memory' learning, like riding a bicycle.

People who have not yet had the experience of drumming in a group or who have never played other forms of transcendent improvised music may doubt the impact of such an apparently simple activity on social awareness or personal identity. Many among us have accepted unfortunate cultural messages that 'music is for experts' or that 'music is for performance and entertainment', leaving our participation in group music limited to singing Happy Birthday and our various national anthems. But tribal societies value music in ways we might emulate for our own benefit. Every drumming gathering metaphorically creates its own 'tribe', with group membership quickly accessible through a willingness to join in. Once we have taken a seat in the circle, we have many ways to affirm our relationship to the group. We can play parts modelled by others and we can use our body intelligence to feel the pulse of the rhythms and play along with the pulse as we experience it. We will discover whether our experience is conventional, common and confirmed by our peers, or whether we truly 'march to a different drummer' and perceive the music in unconventional ways. This feedback will influence our playing, so that a social transformation may occur entirely unconsciously.

But if community drumming experiences were only useful for becoming better musicians, drumming would be of less interest to therapists and counsellors. The powerful social lessons of drumming can be translated into verbal metaphors that apply to social interactions in wide areas of life having nothing to do with music. This is the great achievement that Simon Faulkner is sharing with us; he has honed the language to its essentials, and he presents us with an elegant and orderly entrée into this integrated world, where un-reflected musical experience meets the verbal messages that permit the generalisation of social lessons into the whole fabric of a person's life. A drummer who learns to play more unselfishly becomes a more unselfish person. A drummer who learns that his or her drumming has an important place in the group's overall sound grows in self-worth. A drummer who finds an outlet for his or her painful life experiences in music has less need to harbour these pains or inflict them on others. These kinds of transformational statements are all supported by years of careful research that was either pioneered or inspired by Simon Faulkner. His talents as an educator make his descriptions of this work transparently clear. His experience as a counsellor helps him patiently sequence the material to build from foundations of trust to higher levels of risk and exposure. And having been a musician who started from humble beginnings, he knows how to make the physical coordination demands of the drumming gentle enough to be inclusive and broad enough to accommodate players whose virtuosity can shine.

In a thorough and insightful way, using the highly engaging medium of community drumming, Simon Faulkner has created in Rhythm2Recovery a sequenced model for imparting social awareness to a variety of populations not readily reached by more common counselling methods. His activities are simple to understand, meticulously researched and powerfully impactful in lasting ways. It is my sincere hope that readers put aside any preconceived notions they may have about drumming being a trivial, disorderly or superficial use of therapy time. What the open-minded reader will find is that drumming can provide a cocoon of safety in which participants can viscerally feel their place of belonging in a group. Rhythm2Recovery uses the best elements of experiential learning to help clients discover what it means to support others with a beat, rhythm or groove and learn the lessons of trust that accompany providing and receiving support. They can experiment with how much of their identity to reveal in a group through their willingness to use solo opportunities, which can take place first through the wordless medium of music and later can be matched with a personal verbal narrative.

As author, Simon has conducted an orchestra, blending the accumulated wisdom of cognitive verbal methodologies with the disarmingly engaging, experiential, non-verbal activities afforded by drumming. The success of this model is proving the quality of his work in a growing number of international settings. Grab a drum, read this book, sit in the circle with him and be amazed at the profoundness of what you painlessly learn about yourself and can impart to others.

Dr James Oshinsky, PhD

James is a psychologist and musician. He teaches both psychology and music improvisation courses at Adelphi University in Garden City, NY (USA). He is the author of *Return to Child*, a book about improvisational music making on all instruments and how to teach improvisation. Dr Oshinsky is on the teaching staff of Music for People, an organisation that has been offering improvisation workshops to the public for 30 years.

ACKNOWLEDGMENTS

The author would like to thank all those who inspired and supported this work and the many individuals who have participated in Rhythm2Recovery programs. Your contributions and wisdom are firmly embedded in this work. Special thanks go out to my family, who have provided the foundation from which this work has grown and the nurturing love that has enabled my interest in this field to develop and thrive.

For information on Accredited Rhythm2Recovery Training Programs visit www.rhythm2recovery.com

Contact: simon@rhythm2recovery.com

INTRODUCTION

In 2002, I was working in a small, community high school, in a regional town in the Wheatbelt region of Western Australia, as a member of the local drug and alcohol support service. My work as a counsellor was targeted at young people with a known history of drug use, criminal behaviour or other risk factors such as family dysfunction or homelessness. A good proportion of those chosen by the school for my groups were local Australian Aboriginal children. Being schooled in a cognitive approach my practice centred on trying to build a trusting relationship with those I worked with and engage them in discussing their thoughts, feelings, behaviours and any other issues that impacted their risk of being drawn into the problematic world of addiction. It was difficult, disheartening work and the level of engagement was often very low, because for these young people naming and then talking about such personal issues was both difficult, painful and confronting.

Coming out of one of these sessions, I ran into a colleague whose role was to liaise between these 'higher risk' students, their families and the school authorities; he knew very well the challenges of working in this field. Asking me how my group had gone I said that 'it was like pulling teeth, trying to engage those guys', and in reply he suggested, 'You should try something with drums – they love them'. That passing comment was a spark that changed my life and led me to incorporate rhythmic music as a major part of my clinical practice. It was the same spark that brought fun and hope back into my sessions, removed much of the resistance I had previously struggled against and provided a platform for healing and recovery at a level I had previously thought unimaginable.

When I was first exposed to the potential of this work, I had never played a hand-drum and had little musical background other than an occasional tinkering on the guitar. Although I appreciate the advantages a trained musician may bring to this work, it is certainly not a prerequisite and in my own case I found it advantageous being less able, not the expert, and thus open to empathising with the challenges many individuals go through when learning something new. The simple and inclusive nature of rhythmic music allowed me to incorporate it into my work and makes it accessible to the vast majority of people. It is one of the most practical, enjoyable and useful tools available today for counsellors and educators to utilise in their practice and brings with it access to new dimensions of individual engagement and psycho-social development.

This manual details a model of practice drawn from 15 years of field testing, professional collaboration and individual feedback. The text has been organised into two sections, one of which details the theory and research, including my own practice experience, behind the model and how that applies to different populations. It also includes advice on the resources required to deliver the material, strategies for successful facilitation and insights into overcoming some of the challenges of implementation, particularly with regard to behaviour. Note that this first section does contain a small number of exercises, not replicated in Part 2, that relate to exploring values and examining power struggles.

The second section details the practical rhythmic exercises, games, analogies and metaphors used in the model and aligns these to the 52 session templates that are included in this resource package. All of these exercise have been refined through repeated use in my own practice, and most can be utilised with people across a wide range of ages (from late childhood up) and who present with a diverse range of issues. This section also includes resources for the practitioner interested in extending their knowledge of this field that examine rhythm-based approaches for specific populations in more detail, as well as the critical area of reflective practice and evaluation.

My main interest is in bringing the rehabilitative effects of music into the lives of people who may otherwise not have experienced it, and my foremost hope is that the material collated here can be used to further that end. The manual has been written not as an academic text, but as a practical guide for counsellors and educators who already have an understanding of the foundations of effective practice. I have also refrained from being too specific about the implementation of these techniques in order to allow each individual practitioner to bring their own expertise and creativity to their delivery, encouraging their own natural style to come through. And allowing them to tailor the material to the needs of the individuals they are supporting.

A Note on the Language Used in this Manual

The potential for this work extends across the therapeutic spectrum and into the educational, corporate development and life-coach professions. It is work that can be used with individuals, families, couples and larger groups, including a full classroom. Thus, defining words like 'therapist', and 'counsellor', etc. are often too narrow. I have chosen 'practitioner' as the word for the individual or team leader delivering support and guidance to those in need, and 'individual' or 'participants' for those on the receiving end of this support, rather than 'clients', as I find this professional term for the people we work with cold, impersonal and unsuitable for the warmth and respect inherent in a helpful therapeutic relationship.

> Rhythm and harmony enter most powerfully into the innermost part of the soul and lay forcible hands upon it, bearing grace with them, so making graceful him who is rightly trained.
>
> *Plato*

A Note on the Session Cards

The card I use for these is Hanno Art Silk 350gsm, which is matt laminated on both sides before the corners are rounded. Where possible, I recommend utilising the services of a professional printer. The cards and certificate can be accessed at www.jkp.com/voucher using the code RHYTHM2RECOVERY

PART 1

THEORY, RESEARCH AND RESOURCES

1

WHY RHYTHM?

 Despite all the many wonders that modern science has endowed us with, we still battle, in our Western societies, a rising tide of psychological distress and social isolation. Here the dominant treatment is to prescribe drugs and talk-based therapies, a response that contrasts markedly with the approach of many other cultures that utilise mindful, non-verbal, rhythmic activities, such as dance and drumming as core parts of their healing traditions.

My first experiences of integrating rhythmic music into my practice were primarily inspired by the motivating and connecting power of music. Where days before, individuals had to be followed up to attend my sessions, now they were waiting at the classroom or office door or sometimes in the car-park wanting to help me unload! The presence of the drums changed the nature of our engagement from formal to fun and allowed us to find a fast, non-verbal connection to each other. As well, the drumming noticeably impacted the way that individuals worked together in the groups I ran, often allowing them to form a supportive team in a short period of time and giving them a sense of belonging and place. Response to rhythm is an almost irresistible impulse that has been utilised across human history as a means to connect people in community, promote collaboration and cooperation, and develop social cohesion – fundamental principles of group survival as well as core elements of therapeutic recovery.

Rhythm is the element of music associated with timing and repetition. Of all musical elements, rhythm is the one that binds people most closely, synchronising elements of the brain, and our emotions. When people talk about being 'in tune with each other' or 'in time with each other', this is what they mean. Rhythm extends well beyond music to encompass all elements of life, from the vibrations of the smallest atom to the cyclical rotations of the universe. Rhythm in this broader sense is denoted as 'any predictable pattern over the course of time'. As practitioners or educators we can use the theme of rhythm to explore many facets of human behaviour and how these synchronise with the rhythms (patterns) of life that contextualise them.

Our earliest experiences of rhythm go back to the womb and the dominant presence of our mother's heartbeat. Studies have shown the foetus at 15 weeks responding to changes in rhythm and, in the third trimester, being able to differentiate rhythmic intonations of the mother's voice (DeCasper *et al.*, 1994). The heartbeat rhythm is used across the Rhythm2Recovery model at tempos aligned to a relaxed body state (60–100 beats per minute). For most of us the womb was a secure place and the heartbeat remains a comforting rhythm that can reduce stress and aid relaxation. Leading trauma advocates hypothesise that the influence of the rhythmic vibrations of the heartbeat on the brainstem and midbrain regions during the time of their formation and organisation in the womb, and across the first years of life, makes a case for the use of similar somatosensory rhythmic interventions for people whose homeostatic systems require realignment (Perry and Hambrick, 2008). Patterned, repetitive rhythmic activities can be found in the healing and mourning rituals – dancing, drumming, swaying and chanting – of all cultures around the world.

With the advent of neuro-imaging technology in the 1980s the use of rhythmic music and exercise in health practice has received increasing support from the scientific establishment. Rhythmic music has been shown to impact areas of the brain closely connected to movement, emotional memory and impulse control. Brainstem neurones have been shown to fire synchronously with tempo, leading to theories that music may modulate a range of brainstem-mediated areas, such as our heartbeat rate and blood pressure levels; and in so doing, may be utilised to assist in the regulation of stress and arousal (Chanda and Levitin, 2013). With stress now at unprecedented levels, and music widely recognised as a common alleviator of the condition, this additional research is not before time.

Leading trauma authorities have now incorporated rhythmic exercises, including music and movement, into their recommendations for effective treatment in response to evidence linking rhythm to the realignment of homeostatic states disrupted through ongoing activation of the brain's stress response (Perry and Hambrick, 2008; Van Der Kolk, 2014). Musical rhythm and tempo likely affect central neurotransmissions that maintain cardiovascular and respiratory control, motor function and potentially even higher order cognitive functions (Chanda and Levitin, 2013). Impacting these primal areas of the brain allows rhythmic music to heal beyond the reach of words.

1.1 Rhythm, Repetition and Learning

Since the beginning of recorded human history, repetition, a core element of rhythm, has been at the heart of learning. In ancient Greece, Aristotle highlighted the role of repetition in learning by saying 'it is frequent repetition that produces a natural tendency'. In all areas of learning, repetition and practice are central to levels of attainment and skill (Campitelli and Gobet, 2011). Learning through repetition works because of the way it impacts the brain, strengthening neural connectivity through a process called myelination, which coincides with the development of specific cognitive functions, including memory (Mabbot *et al.*, 2006). The importance of repetition extends to learning new behaviours, through repeated observations and practice, and enhanced by self-corrective adjustment based on feedback of performance.

In the Rhythm2Recovery model the use of rhythmic music and movement provides reinforcement for higher order cognitive learning. The repetitive stimuli of drumming elicits increased levels of focus and attention and, when paired with a learning objective such as social awareness, can improve the level of response (comprehension). We see advertisers taking advantage of this principle every day to maintain customer focus. Exercises in the Rhythm2Recovery program, in which vocal affirmations of self-worth, or behaviour change, are made on top of a regular rhythm, utilise this function. The pairing of rhythmic music and movement to reflective discussions on social and emotional learning develops a reinforcing association between the pleasure, focus and motivation that music engenders and important psycho-social learning concepts that might otherwise be challenging and lead to individuals withdrawing from therapy.

1.2 Rhythm as a Metaphor for Life

Rhythm permeates every aspect of life; we are rhythmic beings living in a rhythmic universe.

As such, rhythm provides the perfect metaphor for describing life and the way it interacts in all its complexity. Rhythms are patterns, and patterns (including habits and routines) dominate human behaviour. Metaphors are used to enhance the therapeutic encounter and can assist in both containing and extending emotional awareness. The use of metaphors is also an avenue for increasing the safety an individual feels when discussing sensitive issues, by substituting and reframing personal experiences and helping individuals tolerate aversive feelings that they may experience on their journey of self-understanding. Using metaphor allows us to create a safe space where the individual/s can explore their own story, test their intuition, their ideas and their judgment, and from there, safely and sensitively explore topics that later can be discussed more openly, outside of the privileged world of storytelling (Lou, 2008).

In the Rhythm2Recovery model this metaphor can be explored in dimensions limited only by the facilitator's imagination and its relevance to the needs of the individual/s they are working with, including:

- rhythms/patterns that are healthy
- rhythms/patterns that are dangerous
- rhythms/patterns of strength
- rhythms/patterns of deceit
- rhythms/patterns that conflict
- rhythms/patterns of stress and anxiety
- rhythms/patterns that are in balance with each other
- rhythms/patterns in nature
- rhythms/patterns of comfort and security
- rhythms/patterns of fear and distress
- rhythms/patterns in our communication

using a Rhythm as a metaphor to describe a life cycle (rythm) that creates one of these feelings

- rhythms/patterns in our parenting

- rhythms/patterns in leadership

- rhythms/patterns of conformity

- rhythms/patterns of rebellion.

The list goes on…

See Section 15.2: A Life in Rhythm for more detail on the use of these analogies.

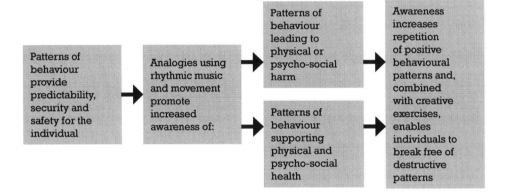

2

THE RHYTHM2RECOVERY MODEL

The Rhythm2Recovery format is an integrative model of practice combining experiential therapy techniques with cognitive behavioural therapy (CBT) influenced by the third-wave approaches of Acceptance and Commitment Therapy (ACT) and Positive Psychology (PP). These newer cognitive approaches are strength based and focus less on exploring problems and more on finding solutions. Although the Rhythm2Recovery model owes much to the influence of these new cognitive approaches, it differs critically in the weight it gives to the role of thoughts in influencing behaviour. Developmental and neuro-imaging studies show that for many people who enter therapy, highly active primal brain areas (limbic system, brainstem) are driving behaviour, while the thinking, rational part of our brains (frontal lobes) are less active (Van Der Kolk, 2014).

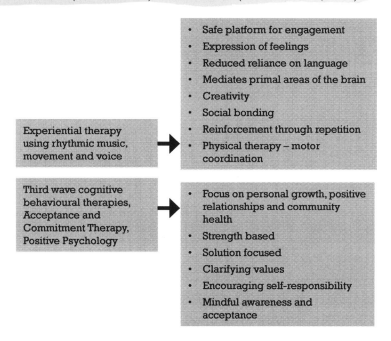

The use of rhythmic music (drums and percussion), rhythmic movement and song make up the experiential elements of a Rhythm2Recovery program, with exercises designed to deliver physical and psycho-social benefits whilst concurrently exploring universal life-skill themes. These experiential exercises are then combined with reflective discussions utilising a cognitive-behavioural framework. This combination increases awareness and focus, expanding perspective and understanding and empowering personal growth. The program materials offer a large degree of flexibility for the practitioner to adapt the content of any specific session to the needs of a wide range of individuals or groups.

The Rhythm2Recovery approach is predominantly psycho-social, exploring the interaction of individual psychology with the social environment. The strength-based, solution-orientated focus of the Rhythm2Recovery model avoids the powerlessness often associated with diagnosis and the defensiveness triggered by examining too closely the personal challenges faced by an individual. A strength-based approach also reduces the likelihood of re-traumatisation that may occur when the focus turns to an individual's problems or pathology. The focus on strengths and solutions also allows the program to be utilised in both clinical and educational contexts. Psycho-social education, often termed social and emotional learning (SEL), is now a key element of school-based education and a mandatory curriculum unit in many school districts – it is closely associated with improved school climate, reduced levels of anti-social behaviour and increased academic performance (Durlak *et al.*, 2011).

Key elements of ACT are incorporated into the Rhythm2Recovery model, including the practise of mindfullness aligned with an accompanying drumming pulse. Mindfulness serves as an ongoing practice for greater awareness and a way to create a separation between the individual and the burden of their unhelpful thoughts. The focus on working with, accepting and detaching from some of the more challenging parts of ourselves (including emotional pain) rather than trying to banish them altogether is a clear principle of ACT that is developed through mindfulness. The other strong synergy with ACT in the Rhythm2Recovery model is our focus on values: that through identifying what is important and meaningful for individuals we uncover a template for action and behaviour.

Positive Psychology focuses on wellbeing and life satisfaction, avoiding negative emotions and symptom relief, and instead focusing on developing and applying individual strengths to everyday issues. PP looks for the positive elements in life to build self-esteem, optimism, resilience, vitality and positive relationships. Each of these different elements impacts how we live and how satisfied we are with our lives (Seligman, 2011). In the Rhythm2Recovery model we incorporate this framework via a strong focus on the influence of healthy, supportive relationships. And by combining engagement with rhythmic music to the use of analogies, drawn from the rhythm exercises, we can explore the benefits of a positive, optimistic, strength-based approach to managing our lives.

Within the Rhythm2Recovery model the term 'Recovery' refers to supporting people to improve the quality of their daily lives. In keeping with the principles of ACT we are not looking to remove symptoms but rather to reduce their influence so that life can be lived fully and meaningfully. More specifically, this model focuses on positive relationships as central to recovery, health and happiness. In fact, social relationships are the single most important factor in our overall quality of life. The exercises contained in the Rhythm2Recovery syllabus address a wide range of different themes that impact our connection to each other. They encourage the development of social and emotional competencies, and understanding, as a way to nurture trusting, equitable and supportive relationships, and as a pathway to sustainable recovery.

Core elements of the Rhythm2Recovery model include a focus on:

- safety – exercises promote a safe therapeutic environment and examine the importance of safety in everyday life and healthy relationships

- values – helping people identify what really matters to them in order to find direction and provide a compass for behaviour

- belonging – music serves as a pathway to connection; exercises explore avenues to social acceptance and community engagement

- self-awareness – mindful awareness allows us to reflect on our thoughts, feelings and behaviours without being beholden to them

- self-responsibility and social responsibility – responsibility allows us to take control of our own lives and work well with others

- positive relationships – exercises foster the relational skills necessary to develop supportive, healthy and respectful relationships with others

- emotional regulation – musical exercises focusing on tempo and volume impact regulatory parts of the brain to assist in the development of improved regulatory skills

- altruism – exercises and activities promote the rewards of giving to and supporting others.

The blend of this approach stems predominantly from my own experiences in working as a counsellor across different settings and the published research drawn from many of those sessions that examined levels of engagement and therapeutic outcomes. My experience in the drug and alcohol, mental health and justice sectors gave me an appreciation of the 'risk factors' and 'protective factors' that influence an individual's trajectory in avoiding, or not, problems of addiction, anxiety, depression or criminal offending; many of the focus areas of the Rhythm2Recovery program are aligned to this research literature. Key to the successful implementation of any model are the skills and reflective practice of the practitioner – their ability to create a safe therapeutic environment, connect genuinely with the individuals they work with, help them find their own truth and motivate them to act in their own interests. In terms of effective practice, a model is at best a template. Practice by its own definition alludes to ongoing learning and adaption. In my mind, effective practice is always individual centred and overrides the demands and constraints of any theory.

2.1 Clarifying Values

In Rhythm2Recovery interventions, assisting people to clarify their values is central to the way we help develop motivation and optimism and sets a course for individual action into the future. Values are a pillar of identity and help people narrow their focus in terms of both therapeutic and life-long goals.

Many people are confused by the term 'values' and have great difficulty pinning down and defining what is of primal importance to them. In my experience this is generally not a process that happens overnight but one that requires regular application, and in fact it is common to see values shift through an individual's time in therapy.

One important opportunity to assist people with exploring their values is to examine their boundaries. When we set up guidelines or boundaries in the first session of an intervention, we can often tie these into looking at values, as the two are intrinsically connected. Boundaries can be seen as markers of our values, delineating what, and what not, is acceptable behaviour.

Two other exercises that are used in the Rhythm2Recovery program to assist people with this process are: 'What Does a Good Friend Do?' and 'What Do You Want from Your Life?'. The former is generally for younger children, while the latter works well for adolescents through to adults.

What Does a Good Friend Do? Part 1

The individual or group should be asked to consider the types of things good friends do for each other; sometimes examples can be offered, such as look out for each other, listen to each other, share with each other, etc.

The group plays a simple foundation rhythm (e.g. B,O,B,O – see Section 10.6 for an explanation of the drumming tablature), over which the practitioner plays a rhythm phrase that symbolises that question: fl–O–o–O–o–fl (What does a good friend do?), addressing one member of the circle at a time. Often when I do this, the whole group joins in with the rhythmic question phrase. At the end of that phrase the rhythm stops and the chosen individual can answer that question with one of three sounds – one Bass note, two Bass notes or three Bass notes. The number corresponds to how many different things they can think of – so if they have one thing they can think of that a good friend does, they answer with one Bass note. After they answer with their drum, they state their example, and then the foundation rhythm resumes.

In group practice only one person answers at a time, and each member of the group answers in succession.

1 + 2 + 3 + 4 +	1 + 2 + 3 + 4 +
B O B O	B O B O
1 + 2 + 3 + 4 +	1 + 2 + 3 + 4 +
Fl OoO o	Fl

These contributions can then be written on a white-board and explored further in relation to 'What does a good person do?' and 'What matters most?', which becomes the second part of the exercise.

What Does a Good Friend Do? Part 2

This time the practitioner refers back to the conversation on 'what good friends do' and 'what good people do' and asks the individual/s to think about 'what matters most to them'. I play the rhythm fl–O–o–O–o–fl (symbolising 'What matters most to you?') and they answer in one of the three ways used before – one Bass note, two Bass notes or three Bass notes. Following their answer on the drum, they can tell the group what's really important to them.

1 + 2 + 3 + 4 +	1 + 2 + 3 + 4 +
Fl OoO o	Fl

Again, write these on the white-board and expand through open-ended questioning.

In group work you will often get people with widely different capacities for responding to these questions, but for those who cannot generate answers, listening to others respond can be helpful in working through their own ideas.

What Do You Want From Your Life?

This exercise follows a similar format, with a preliminary discussion on what matters to the individuals and what they want to get from their lives.

Over the top of a basic foundation rhythm, the practitioner plays a rhythm phrase that symbolises the question 'What do you want from your life?': fl-OoO-OoO (this is also a good exercise to practise triplets – sets of three notes). As in the previous exercise, the individual or group members can answer that question with one of three sounds – one Bass note, two Bass notes or three Bass notes, and the number corresponds to how many different things they can think of. After answering with their drum, the responder states their answer/s and the rhythm resumes.

1 + 2 + 3 + 4 +	1 + 2 + 3 + 4 +
Fl OoO Oo	O

These answers can be written on the white-board for further discussion after the exercise has been completed.

After this initial question, further rounds (sometimes in future sessions) are initiated with new questions:

- Round 2 – What do you want from your relationships?

- Round 3 – What do you want from your job?

- Round 4 – What do you want for your health?

For further values-related exercises see Section 12.2.1.

2.2 Utilising Moral Dilemma Scenarios to Define Values

Another useful way to assist young people or adults to define their values – what they truly believe in – is to use moral or ethical dilemma scenarios that require them to consider a particular challenging situation and examine the way they would act. All of us face these difficult decision-making situations across our lives. Practising these in a theoretical context that is safe can help people respond with confidence when similar situations arise in real life. Moral reasoning helps define values, helping to make our choices clearer and our actions more purposeful.

In the Rhythm2Recovery model we initially ask participants to respond to different moral education scenarios using the 'rumble'. For example, your best friend is cheating on his wife or girlfriend: rumble if you would ask him to stop; rumble if you would ask him to tell his wife; rumble if you would tell his wife yourself; rumble if you would just let it be. These answers are then followed by more formal discussions that examine the ethical dilemmas faced in the story, looking at the implications of different decisions and actions and seeing the consequences through the eyes of others impacted by the same event.

2.2.1 Moral Scenario Examples

- Drugs – You discover a good friend is using and dealing illegal drugs. What should you do? Does it make a big difference that it's your close friend? What about the type of drug – would that make a difference? What else would influence your actions in this case?

- The Stolen Car – Your cousin tells you he and his friends have stolen a car and are going to change the plates, respray it and then sell it. He wants you to check it out – come for a ride. What should you do? Are you an accessory to this crime if you do nothing? How could you get out of this situation? Should you go for the ride? Should you turn in your cousin?

- The Swollen River – It is late afternoon and getting dark; the river is raging – a very fast current. Stuck on a snag 20 metres from the bank is: a $50 note: are you going in? A $100 note: are you going in? Your baby sister or niece: are you going in?

- The Desert – Two people are crossing the desert when their car breaks down; they now have to walk to the next town. They have enough water for the trip if they are careful, but one of them drinks his share very quickly; now they only have enough for one to make it. Would you share your remaining water if you had been careful with it? What if that person was your best friend or a very close family member? Where does self-responsibility come into play here?

- The Transplant – You are approached by your doctor to consider giving up one of your kidneys to help a young boy with kidney disease. You are not related to the boy but have the right blood type and without the kidney the boy may die. Do you give up your kidney? Who would you talk to about this? Would you want to meet the young boy? Should the doctor have asked you in the first place?

- The Cyclone Shelter – There is a level five cyclone approaching your small town and only one person has a cyclone shelter strong enough to withstand the wind, but it is not big enough for everyone to fit in. How would you decide who gets in or not? What about if you were stopped from entering?

- Self-Defence – A man has had his business robbed several times and can no longer get insurance to protect his goods. He sleeps in the shop at night and one evening the thieves try to break in again. This time the man hits them over the head with a baseball bat as they enter, causing them serious injury. Was the man's action justified? Should he be charged with assault? How much responsibility should the thieves accept?

- Drunk Driver – A woman is pulled over for a breath test and found to be just over the limit. The policeman recognises her as his neighbour, a single mum living away from public transport who will struggle a lot without her car. He also knows she drinks regularly. Should he fine her or let her go with a warning?

- The Shoplifter – While shopping at the supermarket, you see a friend of yours get caught by the store manager for trying to steal some food. You know your friend is often hungry, as his parents are unemployed and often there no food in his family's refrigerator. How do you act? Is it OK for your friend to steal in order to eat? If the store manager knew the boy's circumstances, might it change how he acted?

Music can minister to minds diseased, pluck from the memory a rooted sorrow, raze out the written troubles of the brain, and with its sweet oblivious antidote, cleanse the full bosom of all perilous stuff that weighs upon the heart.

William Shakespeare (1564–1616)

3

INDIVIDUAL, FAMILY AND GROUP APPLICATIONS

Many of the exercises detailed in this manual are adaptable to individual, family and group settings. The vast majority of counsellors work with individuals, and introducing Rhythm2Recovery exercises can add a new and engaging dimension to the often confronting process of traditional 'issue-focused' verbal therapy. In the counselling room the drum is an item of interest that can serve as a tool for connection and dialogue. Often individuals enter the room and the first thing they notice is the drum. This provides me with an opening for engagement that doesn't immediately confront them with the pain and shame behind their visit. Adults are often intrigued by the drum and its connection to counselling, and I sometimes talk to them about the part music has played in traditional healing historically, as well as some of the latest neurological research findings supporting such practice. This provides some context and helps move them gently towards the idea of utilising the instrument for this purpose; for the sceptic however, this may not be useful. Sometimes I purposefully allow the individual into the therapy room containing the drums some minutes before I enter, often to find them tapping away quite contentedly. I find that when I do this, much of their anticipatory tension leaves the room, and before any any talking starts I often join them in their rhythm – introducing myself and connecting to them non-verbally.

For specific individuals who are challenging to engage verbally or who have significant cognitive deficits (see Chapter 4 on working with specific populations) drumming may take up a whole session, utilising exercises that address the release of feelings, communication, regulation and emotional awareness. More common, however, is the intermittent use of Rhythm2Recovery experiential exercises for specific purposes, alongside the practitioner's preferred model of practice. I have found that a consistent approach that utilises the musical exercises at specific points of a session (e.g. opening – rhythm exercise promoting collaboration and release of feelings; mid-way – key exercise related to a specific issue being addressed in the session; closing – free expression and release of feelings) is often well received and effective in reducing the monotony and pressure of continual question and answer dialogue.

Rhythmic-based exercises and programs drawn from the Rhythm2Recovery catalogue have also been utilised by a range of agencies working with families. The use of the musical components of the model have helped reduce the level of resistance from family members who may be there against their will. The relational content of many of the Rhythm2Recovery sessions lends itself to exploring the inter-personal dynamics of family systems, particularly around communication and teamwork issues. In my work with families I have also noticed a reduction in how problematic power dynamics, embedded in language, affect the session, due I suspect to the fact that all members are forced to work through a new medium and hence find themselves on a level playing field.

In sessions with foster children and their foster parents, the use of rhythmic music has been useful in developing a positive connection and restoring a level of trust for those whose ability to trust has previously been fractured. Playing music has been shown to release a number of neural peptides associated with increased levels of empathy and social bonding and has long been associated with improved social cohesion and trust (Levitin, 2009). Again, the relational content of the Rhythm2Recovery material and the teamwork required to complete the exercises assists the practitioner and individuals they work with to identify areas of strength, as well as conflict and dysfunction, and to initiate measures to develop or address these; all within a fun-focused medium that helps temper frustrations.

The majority of my work has been spent as a group counsellor and I confess that I lean towards group facilitation as a preferred method when it comes to psycho-social approaches. This is because so much of psycho-social education comes down to the contextual application of the learning, and groups provide us with a more realistic social context. There is increasing recognition amongst specialists in the behavioural field of the social advantages of group work, particularly for isolated individuals who have lost the skills and self-confidence necessary for pro-social interaction. In leaning towards group work, however, I also recognise that many individuals are not suitable, or ready, to join a group and will benefit more from one-to-one therapy. Placing these individuals in groups without some form of suitability assessment prior to entering can seriously undermine the potential of the group process.

In delivering the Rhythm2Recovery sessions to groups there is a great deal of flexibility when it comes to the options before the practitioner. Most people will implement a series of sessions drawn from one of the five core themes available in the 'session card pack' (see link on p.15) that makes up part of this resource. However, there are many other occasions where just a brief intervention is required, or simply a single session, to address a specific issue. If working with groups, then group size is also flexible, and can be anywhere from a minimum of six participants to a full classroom or large group of up to 30 participants. It is important to note that, generally, group safety and individual therapeutic outcomes decline as group numbers rise, with optimum group size ranging from 8 to 12 participants, excluding facilitators.

Critical Considerations for Effective Groups

- A suitable venue – group drumming can be loud and disturb others, and requires an open space with reasonable acoustic properties, free from distracting elements and clutter.

- Hearing protection – Provide earplugs or headphones for people sensitive to loud noise.

- Pre-group assessment – For therapeutic groups it is essential to screen for students or adults whose behaviours are likely to undermine or sabotage the group process (see Section 6.3 on managing difficult behaviours).

- A similarity in developmental capacity – Many groups are undone by the challenges of meeting the needs of members who are at significantly different developmental levels and thus require quite different approaches.

- Group facilitation skills – Group facilitation is an acquired skill requiring training and practice; those new to the medium should consider co-facilitation with a more experienced practitioner.

- Confidentiality – What is said in the group stays in the group. In some groups (youth groups or those in small communities) it is best to assume a lack of confidentiality and avoid sensitive personal disclosures altogether.

- Feedback and supervision – Providing opportunities for participant feedback and regular supervision by an experienced colleague will help develop a more appropriate alignment between individual expectations and program outcomes, and also improve facilitation technique.

4

WORKING WITH SPECIFIC POPULATIONS

The Rhythm2Recovery model has been designed to allow the practitioner to adapt the material to the needs of the different individuals they work with, as rhythmic music has benefits across the age spectrum, genders and with people from all cultures facing a myriad of physical, psychological and social challenges. Practitioners themselves have different personalities, strengths, levels of experience and qualifications and most tend to find an area of specialty that suits their temperament and skill-set. However, it is not unusual, in this competitive age, for people to work in multiple settings and to be asked to extend their practice into new areas.

Over the past 15 years I have worked with diverse groups of individuals in a wide range of settings and seen first hand how adaptive this resource can be. I have also trained many professionals from different backgrounds in rhythmic modalities, encouraging each to adapt these techniques in response to the needs of the different individuals or groups they work with. The following information details some key issues when working with specific populations and is drawn from feedback from my colleagues working in these areas with rhythm and my own personal experience.

4.1 Early Childhood

Early childhood is generally recognised as the years following infancy, between the ages of three and eight years of age, and is a critical developmental period that has implications for an individual's wellbeing across the life span. At this age, rhythm games using music, movement and song assist with a wide range of developmental attributes including motor coordination, balance, language acquisition, socialisation, motivation and cognitive and intellectual growth. Rhythm games are a useful resource for the early childhood educator or practitioner, facilitating learning through play and helping young children learn key social skills as they interact with others, including how to regulate their own behaviour and emotions.

Key Tips for Maximising Engagement and Learning Outcomes for this Age Group

- Create a safe play space with plenty of room for movement. Ensure musical instruments provided are child-safe. Ensure children feel safe, welcome and accepted.

- Allow children relative freedom in choosing and playing their instruments – provide a range of appropriate small drums and percussion. Don't get fixated on harmony or rules.

- Align activities to the children's developmental level – reduce the discussion element and focus on the experiential process. Keep rhythms and songs simple and repetitive.

- Encourage all appropriate communication between children, and between children and staff – use music as a form of communication (e.g. call and response). Role-model appropriate social behaviour, sharing, etc.

- Maximise the use of repetition to ingrain learning.

- Maximise levels of encouragement.

Practical Exercises for this Age Group

- Guessing games such as 'What Sound Was That?' 12.1.4(f).

- Mimicking games such as 'Call and Response' 12.1.1 or 'Copy That' 16.2(c), which promote attending skills.

- Well-known songs that can be sung to a simple rhythm and incorporate body movement, such as 'If You're Happy and You Know It' – adapt this song to include playing different instruments as a sign of happiness: 'If you're happy and you know it, play your drum.'

- Songs and exercises that feature emotions, such as 'You Are My Sunshine'. Play different instruments to represent different emotions, as in 'A Storm of Feeling' 16.1(c).

- Counting games such as 'How Many Beats?' 16.5(b).

- Creative rhythm games such as 'Make Up Your Own' 12.6.5(b) where young people make up their own rhythm patterns and the other children play along with them.

4.2 Individuals with Special Needs

Individuals with special needs, those with mental, physical, social or emotionally delayed development, fall into such a broad range of categories or diagnoses that making generalised recommendations regarding a therapeutic approach becomes problematic and potentially misleading. However, special needs programs are now common in education and health systems across the world and many of the exercises and techniques in the Rhythm2Recovery model have broad application for these populations. Music is a powerful tool for the special needs facilitator, who can harness it to assist in the development of a wide range of social and emotional skills through a fun and flexible medium. Specific exercises in the Rhythm2Recovery catalogue can address areas such as impulse control, coordination and balance, eye contact, transitions, sound localisation, emotional awareness, group interaction, attention and focus levels and social skills such as sharing, turn-taking and communication (see Chapter 12).

One of the most common issues facing special needs populations, particularly those on the autism spectrum, is a lack of emotional awareness, which impacts their ability to reciprocate appropriately with others on a social and emotional level. There are many fun Rhythm2Recovery exercises that focus specifically on emotional attunement, using music as a language of emotional connection. In these exercises the drum is played by the practitioner at a volume and tempo that replicates a specific level of emotional intensity, and the individual or group are asked to replicate it on their own instrument, passing these different emotional representations amongst themselves, with the receiver focusing on aligning their response to what is directed their way.

A critical consideration when working with individuals with special needs is the need for flexibility and adaption in our interactions, particularly in the way we attend and respond to the needs of different individuals, recognising that in a special needs classroom, or when working with different individuals, each person will require a different blend of strategies to facilitate engagement and learning. Flexibility means not getting locked into our expectations of what we might achieve in any one session and always having alternative options if our current plan is not working.

Other Vital Points for Working with Music in this Area

- Creating a safe environment – For many people with special needs, safety means stability and consistency. Regular routines help reduce anxiety that often develops quickly in the face of too many new experiences. Routine greeting and departing exercises provide a level of structural certainty in a music session. Routine and consistency don't mean a lack of creativity and challenge – in fact, for many people with high-functioning autism simple rhythms can exacerbate behavioural problems due to boredom (Strong, 2015).

- Observe, interact and communicate – Many individuals with special needs are challenged verbally and socially. It is important for facilitators to observe the different ways individuals with special needs communicate both their desires and anxieties, and to find pathways to interact and communicate with them. In particular, they should leave adequate time for responding and use musical exercises such as 'Call and Response' 12.1.1 and 'Rumbles' 12.1.2 to facilitate non-verbal communication. Group music making is a safe form of social communication and for individuals who face challenges in this area participation enables many different social interaction skills to be targeted and developed.

- Be alert to sensory sensitivities, particularly in relation to sound – Many individuals with special needs have trouble with sensory integration and can experience sensory overload in response to noise levels that others find relatively benign. Providing headphones or earplugs can help avoid this, as can introducing the sound gradually to allow a build up of tolerance. Tactile sensitivities are also common within these populations, and some materials such as drum skins may cause distress. Offering alternative instrument choices, gloves or opportunities for brief exposure can assist with this issue.

- Identify the learning preferences of your participants – There are three major ways people learn (visual, auditory and kinaesthetic) and most have a strength or preference for one particular mode (Biggs 2001). Use different strategies to support individuals with different learning preferences. Visual references such as written rules for respectful behaviour or hand signals for stop and start are helpful for visual learners – many autistic children have strong visual memories. Auditory cues such as calls on the drum or other percussion instruments can be useful in gaining attention and signalling transitions for auditory learners, and respectful touch can be useful in assisting those who favour tactile communication, particularly in the learning of new rhythms.

- Stay positive – Working with special needs can be exhausting and quickly lead to frustration and negativity. Special needs facilitation requires patience and a generous attitude, which can be vulnerable when we enter into the relationship with too much judgment and too many expectations. As much as possible, we need to be present – in the moment – for those we are supporting, ensuring we have the support we need and maintaining a positive and encouraging attitude.

In general the themed sessions detailed on the Rhythm2Recovery resource cards are inappropriate for populations with special needs, and the practitioner is best directed to utilise or adapt games from the 'Themes and Exercises' sections (see Section 12) that promote engagement at the appropriate developmental level and address the issues most relevant to those they are supporting.

4.3 Youth

Most of my work over the past 15 years has been with young people between the ages of 10 and 18 – young people who have often been classified as 'at risk' and who exhibit challenging behaviours and are often disconnected from mainstream society. This age period is a challenging one for any young person, and I find many of the generalisations applied to 'young people these days' unhelpful and disrespectful. In saying that, however, most of the young people who find their way into my groups face above average and often overwhelming challenges.

I've always regarded this work as a privilege, given the potential for learning and change that exists at this age, and I have been lucky enough to witness significant shifts in social confidence, social connection and life direction on numerous occasions. Young people generally bring with them a real passion for music, as it remains a critical part of youth culture, contributing significantly in the development of self-identity and as a source of emotional support, a mood regulator and a source of community (Zillman and Gan, 1997). Most young people, however, still have little chance to play music on a regular basis. To be able to assist them to develop from passive listeners to confident musicians, whilst fostering the attendant personal development outcomes, is a wonderful motivator for any practitioner.

Working with disaffected young people often has its challenges, and like most people who work in this field I have had times where I felt disillusioned and frustrated. Most of this frustration is born out of one major issue that can generally be circumvented with proper preparation and a genuinely positive attitude: that is, how secure and at ease participants feel with the process. Safety is a recurring theme in Rhythm2Recovery therapeutic and educational practice, because it is fundamental to the therapeutic relationship, which remains the best predictor of therapeutic outcomes (Norcross, 2009). Much of the resistance and defiant behaviour that occurs when working with young people is provoked by feelings of threat and the conscious and unconscious defensiveness that arises from it. For young people who have experienced traumatic events, that sense of threat is often locked on permanently as the brain's defensive mechanisms become over-sensitised. Establishing a safe environment for participation is one of the highest priorities for the Rhythm2Recovery facilitator, and it is important to note that for many individuals, young and old, the very act of playing music itself is often threatening.

Feelings of safety or insecurity stem from our earliest experiences of life and the attachment we made with our primary care-giver. Insecure attachment due to inconsistent or unresponsive parenting leads to continuing relational difficulties across the life span. Insecurity and feelings of threat can be caused or exacerbated by a wide range of life circumstances and triggered by many varied, often unpredictable, stimuli. Youth interventions, particularly those targeting 'disaffected' individuals, require facilitators to develop quickly a trusting relationship and to minimise those factors that may provoke a sense of vulnerability or fear.

Strategies to Foster a Sense of Safety

- The genuine positive regard of the practitioner towards each individual – Young people quickly recognise those who pretend to be what they are not. The facilitator treats the young person respectfully and focuses on individual strengths.

- A focus on fun – Using games, humour, positivity and encouragement to keep the mood light and friendly, not getting bogged down in heavy discussions.

- A level of consistency in the sessional format – Same time, place, practitioner, etc.

- Clear boundaries – Defining and enforcing clear boundaries on physical and emotional safety through an inclusive process helps young people identify situations in other walks of life that are unhealthy or present risks.

- Opportunities for empowerment and autonomy – For many young people life is a constant reminder of the lack of power they have over their own lives. The facilitator provides choices, encourages responsibility and offers opportunities for input into, and leadership within, the therapeutic process.

- The environment is secure and conducive to focused learning. This is particularly relevant to groups where peer relationships can strongly impact feelings of security; sessions in juvenile detention centres being a prime example. Consideration of suitable group make up is essential prior to beginning any group process.

- The use of early warnings, or preventative interruption, to safeguard vulnerable young people from disclosing confidential information of a highly personal nature in front of their peers.

- The introduction into music making is paced at a level to foster success and avoid anxiety. An awareness of participants' developmental capacity can assist with this alignment. Instruments and techniques are chosen that are relatively simple to master in the early sessions.

- The emphasis on discussion and communicating in language is minimised in the early sessions and replaced by communication through the drum. Language is prone to misinterpretation. Music as a form of emotional communication has been linked to improved levels of empathy and social bonding (Levitin, 2009).

All of the session themes in the Rhythm2Recovery model are relevant to both adults and young people, but the key program areas of 'Social and Emotional Learning' and 'Strengths and Virtues' are particularly useful for youth and are linked to aspects of the national curriculum. Reflective discussions need to be handled skilfully to maintain engagement; in particular, the facilitator should focus on initially asking questions that can be answered using the drum itself (e.g. 'Rumble if you agree that...'). As confidence increases, open-ended questions that call on personal experiences work best in encouraging youth participation, with the facilitator simplifying any complex language to ensure it is understood and remaining open to allowing the discussion to drift into new areas that are relevant to the lives of the participants.

4.4 Mental Health

Those with a diagnosed mental illness have been amongst the groups of people I have worked with who benefit most from rhythmic music and reflection. Although some people within these populations have an acute sensitivity to sound (particularly those who have experienced psychosis), the vast majority are active participants and report high levels of enjoyment, long-term mood improvement, reduced anxiety and an overall increase in wellbeing (Holyoake Institute, 2009). These findings have recently been supported by researchers in the United Kingdom, who confirmed sustained reductions in levels of depression and anxiety, as well as improvements in social resilience and the immune system for patients participating in weekly drumming compared with a non-drumming control group (Fancourt *et al.*, 2016). In particular, the common symptoms of social anxiety and social isolation are ameliorated by involvement in the group drumming exercises, which promote social connection and a sense of belonging.

When working or socialising with people who are under undue stress, it is often common to see them self-soothing with rhythmic tapping of the hands or feet. This natural response to anxiety, involving a subconscious, sensory search for grounding and stability, can be utilised by practitioners to find practical ways of reducing emotional arousal using conscious rhythmic body tapping. In combination with a focus on the alignment of the breath, the individual is shown regulatory techniques using their own body rhythms (or introducing specific Rhythm2Recovery rhythms that are played on the body at specific tempos) that involve a gradual slowing of tempo and physical intensity and can be utilised whenever or wherever required. These exercises deliver an increased level of agency for the individual over their own emotional response.

In in-patient, out-patient, early discharge units, as well as community mental health settings, drumming programs have been used to assist people with social integration, emotional regulation, mood disorders, depression and anxiety. Studies have demonstrated that rhythmic musical exercises at specific tempos (60–80 bpm) can rapidly develop alpha brainwave states that promote feelings of calm and relaxation, whilst at the same time placing people in a fully immersed state of flow that reduces hyper-vigilant thoughts associated with anxiety (Freidman, 2000). The central, Rhythm2Recovery, mindfulness exercise 'The Rhythmic Wave' (Chapter 11) has been designed to further assist people to reduce the impact of unhelpful thoughts and feelings, reduce stress, stay calm and nurture the self.

Recovery in mental health is a multifaceted process that requires a combination of personal fortitude and social and professional support. Rhythm2Recovery exercises and reflective practice can assist the individual to gain a new sense of personal autonomy by increasing feelings of self-worth, harnessing strengths, increasing optimism and providing opportunities for creative expression. On a social level, these activities can help define and clarify supportive and healthy relationships, improve social and emotional understanding, increase social connection and social acceptance, and reduce emotional vulnerabilities.

Meanwhile, at the physiological level, music and movement exercises can provide aerobic exercise and improve coordination, motor control and balance. Improvements in affect, mood and cognitive functioning (increased levels of focus and concentration) have each been noted after rhythmic-based musical interventions (Holyoake Institute, 2009; Schneck and Berger, 2005).

Most of the key challenges in working with individuals with a mental health issue, or through mental health services, are related to the instability of an individual's health. People with long-term mental illness often present for support at a time when they are most vulnerable to the challenges of their illness. This makes group work, in particular, difficult, as at any one session several people may not attend due to the fluctuating impact of their symptoms. Open groups are preferable in these circumstances, as is having a larger registration of attendees in order to safeguard against absenteeism reducing numbers to the point where the group is no longer viable.

Uses of Rhythm2Recovery exercises

In individual and group sessions in mental health settings we use the Rhythm2Recovery exercises to:

- develop a trusting therapeutic alliance – promoting trust through a shared, non-verbal experience

- identify 'stressors' and 'relaxors' – using 'The Pressure Pot' 12.2.5(a) and 'Pressure Valve' 12.2.5(b) exercises

- teach relaxation in ways that can be useful for many individuals, young and old, and can be used outside the counselling room – breathing, mindfulness and tapping

- explore emotions and emotional control – 'Mirror That Emotion' 16.1(b), 'Emotional Journey' 12.5.4(a) and 'The Rhythmic Wave' exercises (Chapter 11)

- express emotions in a safe context – using 'Show Some Emotion' 12.2.2(a) and the closing exercise 'Free Expression' (Section 4.7)

- maintain optimism – for many individuals, young and old, optimism and hope are in short supply – use 'Accent the Positive 12.2.3(a) and 'The Lookout' 12.4.10

- identify strengths and other personal resources to call upon in aid of recovery – using 'Find Your Strengths' 12.5.8(b)

- examine our social relationships and manage peer pressure, particularly in relation to unhealthy behaviours such as problematic drug use – using 'Friends' 12.3.3(a), 'Hold Onto Your Rhythm' 11.1 and 'Hold Onto Your Values 12.2.1

- express oneself and explore our identity, hopes and dreams – using 'Make Up Your Own' 12.6.5(b) and 'Rumble If You Hope To' 12.5.6(a).

Of the different sessional themes presented in this resource package – the 'Social and Emotional' learning cards and those of the 'Health and Wellbeing' pack are most relevant to the needs of this population.

4.5 Alcohol and Drug Users

People struggling with problems related to alcohol and drug use often present with similar issues to those with a mental health diagnosis, as the two conditions often coexist. Research literature in the drug and alcohol field highlights a range of 'protective factors' that help protect an individual from succumbing to problems of addiction. Amongst these are some of the key objectives of the Rhythm2Recovery model, including a strong connection to community, healthy social relationships and positive self-regard (Pollard, Hawkins and Arthur, 1999). In addition, the latest research on addiction confirms that drugs and alcohol themselves play a relatively minor role in determining whether someone maintains problematic use. Life factors, including personal histories of trauma, poverty and social isolation, are the primary determinants – 'Drug abuse is a disease of loneliness' (Dean Wilson, quoted in Hari, 2015).

The subject themes in the Rhythm2Recovery model address a number of 'risk factors' identified as increasing the likelihood of problematic use (Pollard *et al.*, 1999). High amongst these is the negative influence of peers and family members who encourage substance misuse. For many people dealing with addiction issues, the greatest challenge is to break with those people closest to them who encourage or in some other way enable their use to continue. Increasing this challenge is the fact that often these same people provide the affected individual with their only avenue for social support and belonging. Drug and alcohol use often starts as a social lubricant but eventually leads to chronic social isolation. Group programs, and recreational drumming, offer people the opportunity to enter new social circles where they can find additional support or simply a place to unwind and connect to others in safety.

A number of studies have showcased the potential of drumming interventions as complementary therapies (Slotoroff, 1994; Winkleman, 2003). These examples reinforce the potential of drumming to assist people to connect to others, express feeling and emotions, and reduce levels of hyper-vigilance, whilst at the same time increasing levels of calm. The Rhythm2Recovery template expands these outcomes to incorporate cognitive learning relevant to addiction through relational topics such as peer pressure, social support, healthy relationships, values and self-responsibility.

Rhythmic music releases a number of neurochemical transmitters into the body that deliver high levels of arousal, pleasure and emotional intensity, in much the same way that many drugs do, acting on the opioid, cortisol, serotonin and oxytocin systems. Music can also regulate the release of chemicals that are associated with arousal and anxiety, reducing their level whilst at the same time modulating heart rate and blood pressure rate to reduce worry and stress (Chanda and Levitin, 2013). For these reasons music has often been called a 'legal high' and can provide the drug user with a healthy alternative for stress and pain relief.

Most interventions with drug and alcohol users and their families focus on the relational content of the 'Social and Emotional Learning' cards and those that examine 'Families, Teams and Communities' and 'Health and Wellbeing'.

4.6 Trauma

There has been an increasing focus on the impact of trauma in recent times, particularly in response to the many thousands of returned servicemen and women who have recently come home from war zones after witnessing horrific events and the high number of civilians fleeing these same conflicts as refugees. Prolonged exposure to traumatic events or abuse is an underlying causal factor for a wide range of human psychological and physiological problems. It is estimated that over 70 per cent of people living with mental health and drug addiction issues have experienced ongoing trauma at some point of their lives and that over 90 per cent of female prisoners have histories of trauma (Kilroy, 2001).

Developments in neuroscience have once again forced clinicians to rethink the way they respond to people living with trauma; and amongst the key understandings awakened by this field is the way in which primitive brain responses govern behaviour beyond the reach of conscious intervention. Guidelines for informed trauma practice, and the recommendations of a wide range of leading trauma authorities, now point to the need to extend therapy beyond the traditional cognitive approach and to include physical therapies that can help regulate the biological stress response (Perry and Hambrick, 2008; Ogden, Minton and Pain, 2006; Van Der Kolk, 2014).

Rhythmic musical exercises that replicate the tempo of the mother's heartbeat (60–100 bpm) are thought to impact positively on the organisation of the brainstem/diencephalon regions of the brain that regulate an individual's response to stress (Perry and Hambrick, 2008). For individuals whose stress response has been over-activated through repeated exposure to fearful events, this part of the brain dominates the way they live; it is locked on and remains overly sensitive to perceived threats (Van Der Kolk, 2014). For these individuals, rational thoughts may not serve to mediate behaviour in response to such threats. Because of the hierarchical nature of brain development, addressing this primal brain region is often a critical first step in therapy for people who are at the mercy of a chronically dysfunctional stress response, preceding cognitive interventions that require higher order processing. I have found slowly paced, repetitive heartbeat exercises extremely useful in developing trust and connection with people whose perpetual state of fear limits their relational ability.

Rhythm2Recovery rhythm exercises have been developed to replicate the soothing and re-orientating tempo of the mother's heartbeat. They provide a sensitive pathway for the practitioner to support the individual, without the danger of re-traumatisation that may occur from more invasive therapy that prematurely examines the traumatic event itself. At the same time, the analogies drawn from the Rhythm2Recovery exercises help individuals clarify and express their thoughts and feelings. Many people suffering from trauma struggle with

'Alexithymia', the inability to articulate feelings, and in giving voice to their thoughts, which are overwhelmed by their emotions (Van Der Kolk, 2014). The mindfulness exercises within the Rhythm2Recovery model and specifically 'The Rhythmic Wave' exercise (Chapter 11) are designed to help manage and modulate an individual's emotional responses, calming the sympathetic nervous system and increasing emotional control.

From my own experience working with traumatised individuals, many of whom were young children, the primary benefit of using rhythmic music was the way in which it enabled people to connect together, tune into each other and develop renewed confidence in their social relationships. For most people, the real impact of their trauma is in how it negatively impacts their relationships. The process of entrainment, the synchronisation of two phenomena, occurs when individuals play music together and generates both a physical and psychological connection that engenders safety and helps pave the way for a restoration of trust.

4.7 Veterans

The presenting issues for veterans are similar to those of people suffering from long-term trauma, with combat stress reaction and post traumatic stress disorder the leading causes of psychiatric illness in returned servicemen and women – affecting about one in every six (Richardson, Frueh and Acierno, 2010). Common symptoms include flashbacks, emotional numbing, anger and frustration, social isolation and loneliness. Drumming programs are now being used to support veterans in many rehabilitation centres around the world, with growing recognition of their potential to address many of the symptoms above. In particular, the stabilising impact of rhythm on the over-sensitised stress response is a critical therapeutic application for this demographic. Drumming provides veterans with a safe, physical medium for the venting of feelings; in our veterans' groups we often talk to participants about their drum being a vessel into which they can release the pent-up frustrations and emotions that may be hiding and building inside them (see 'Emotional Journey' 12.5.4(a)). The physicality of the drumming is often used by veterans as a form of emotional release and it is not unusual for these groups initially to favour fast and furious beats.

Free Expression

Age range: suitable for all ages.

Individuals are allowed to express themselves freely on the drum, with an emphasis on the safe release of feelings, rather than on group harmony; although often over time the two will marry. Opportunities for free expression should be part of every session and are a standard part of the session templates that accompany this text.

Drumming is no stranger to war, with drums having been used in different capacities on the battlefield since our earliest conflicts as human beings. The sound of the drum has the potential to invoke traumatic memories of war and must be handled sensitively. In the groups I have been involved with these associations were clearly present and discussed openly. They did not negatively impact the individuals in the group, who gradually increased their level of acceptance to the sound and the memories it triggered, a process resembling habituation. Drumming over time may help reduce participants' vulnerability to noise-induced trauma reactions (Bensimon, Amir and Wolf, 2008).

Many veterans have issues with social integration – moving back into general community living after years spent in the rarefied atmosphere of a military community. The group work drum-circle replicates this sense of bonding and community that veterans are secure in, but may also represent an obstacle for the practitioner trying to break down the insular tendencies of the veteran support club and help extend social pathways into broader community networks. There is a sense of elitism in many veterans' groups that no one can really understand 'unless you were there'. This same sense of belonging can also mean a sense of rejection towards those outside the 'club' and this topic is often a critical one to raise and explore in these groups, being highly debilitating in terms of social reintegration and often premised on fear.

My colleague Terrie King, who has utilised elements of the Rhythm2Recovery model in her work with veterans in Eastern Texas, has also encountered this strong sense of 'brotherhood' amongst veterans and recommends avoiding mixing non-veteran personnel with these groups due to their reluctance to reveal the true nature of their feelings (sadly often defined as showing weakness) amongst strangers. However, she noted the equal importance of establishing concurrent groups for family members impacted by the return of veterans dealing with trauma.

The constant stress placed on the limbic system by the ongoing physical threat of war has a severe impact on the sleeping patterns of veterans. The mindfulness practice within the Rhythm2Recovery model can be used to reduce hyper-vigilance and help induce calm, supporting better sleep. The use of drumming at specific tempos that align to brainwave states of rest and relaxation (alpha – 40–60 bpm) also has application here.

4.8 Parents

 When researchers study the causes of social problems like juvenile crime, child abuse, teenage pregnancy, substance abuse or truancy, they find parenting implicated as the single most important variable. Good parenting provides a social buffer against these types of issues and mediates the damage when they occur. Though there is widespread debate about what 'good parenting' actually involves, most experts connect it to three spheres – protection from emotional and physical harm, setting and enforcing boundaries to protect from harm and optimising a child's potential by providing warmth, security and appropriate developmental opportunities. Parenting then is a critical public health issue, and parenting programs are a vital prevention strategy – far more likely to be effective than reactive policies implemented in response to social ills.

Working with parents requires a clear assessment and understanding of their needs in relation to the complexities of the issues they present with and in their capacity (including level of confidence) as parents. Many parents present with multiple, complicating factors that impact the child–parent relationship, and only a broad, historical understanding of their issues can assist the practitioner in formulating an appropriate response. Another key factor that can impact the success of a parenting intervention is the parents' own relationship with each other (if two parents exist) and whether that is respectful, intact or antagonistic. Attachment issues for the children, and cultural factors that impact parenting styles and expectations, also need to be taken into account.

Rhythm2Recovery interventions have been utilised in parent counselling, group parenting programs and mixed groups of parents and their children. In particular, the Rhythm2Recovery format has been successful in engaging parents who are resistant to the talk-based formats of most traditional parenting programs and also for including children and adolescents in family-based learning. These mixed groups require the practitioner to monitor relationships between parent and child and intervene to ensure that a safe environment is maintained and power dynamics don't favour one party at the expense of the other – to assist with this, we usually recommend only one parent per child. The topics that make up the ten sessions comprising the 'families, teams and communities' program cover many aspects of family relationships and are easily adapted to target specific parenting concerns.

4.9 Aged Care

Rhythmic music activities offer the elderly many physiological and psychological benefits, combining as they do the physical and the social. Some of the issues that are addressed by the use of rhythmic exercises include mood, memory, social connection, physical balance coordination and motor skills. As individuals age, there are a range of changes that take place physically and cognitively, which need to be recognised and accommodated by the practitioner. These changes are natural and progress with age, but can be mediated in terms of their intensity by many of the Rhythm2Recovery exercises included within this resource.

Physical changes include regressions over time that impact strength and stamina – older people tire more easily after physical activity and also face more challenges completing activities that involve complex motor behaviour. The practitioner can accommodate these realities by ensuring that activities are not overly physical and that the sessions are not overly long, and by including breaks or changes in momentum that allow physical rest. A range of percussion options will allow for individuals to rotate instruments and avoid muscle fatigue associated with playing the same instrument for too long. In the sessions I run with aged populations we move regularly between drums and percussion (often using 'tonal chimes', see Section 9.3), alternating periods of physical energy with contemplative reflection.

Changes also occur over time in our sensory capacity, particularly our hearing, but also our vision and balance. Facilitators must adapt their teaching style, understanding that many older people have difficulty hearing and, to a lesser degree, seeing. As much as possible, keep verbal instructions simple and clear, speaking slowly whilst extending your instructional cues to include clear hand signals for such things as starting and stopping, and make sure you harness everyone's attention and reduce other background noise prior to speaking. Some aged people will react negatively to loud sound such as drumming or bells and must be helped to find a place of comfort within the group where this is minimised.

The ability to learn new things does not recede with age, but may require different strategies. Older people benefit from new experiences and learning, which can help maintain cognitive function, memory and intelligence. The impact of music on the brain and its connection to emotional memory through the amygdala is a powerful conduit for cognitive stimulation. The analogies and metaphors in the Rhythm2Recovery exercises create links that can aid in the recall of memories. Many facilitators use this process to facilitate dialogue with their aged care participants that draws on personal experiences and stories to explore themes relevant to their situation and to stimulate memory (MacTavish, 2012).

The mental health of our ageing population is one of the key issues facing policy makers responsible for this sector, as studies conclude that levels of depression and anxiety are increasing to excessive levels, particularly for those living alone in supported care facilities (Australian Institute of Health and Welfare, 2013). Rhythmic drumming groups assist in reducing these issues by providing an opportunity for fun, physical activity and social connection – all known preventative factors.

Facilitators can help embed these outcomes by maintaining a welcoming, supportive and non-judgmental environment (safety), using qualified staff, volunteers and family members for support, and encouraging group interaction through shared activities and discussion.

The Rhythm2Recovery activities and strategies you utilise for your sessions will very much depend on the demographic of the aged care population you are working with. Most aged care facilitators refrain from implementing a set program, instead combining different exercises and discourses that align with the desires, needs and capacity of the individuals they are working with, and including a strong focus on fun, shared activities and creative self-expression. Prior to implementing any program, it is critical to work with the centre's management to ascertain the level of activities accessible to the group, ensure appropriate carer support and arrange a suitable venue.

4.10 Corporate Management and Staff

Much of the Rhythm2Recovery material is suitable for smaller scale corporate development programs. The relational themes of the Rhythm2Recovery material have clear application to inter-personal dynamics of the workplace and their relationship to efficiency and productivity. In the group music circle, a range of teamwork skills apply and can be examined as the participants work together to create music. The quality of the music that team members make together generally provides insight into their ability to work constructively together. Whilst many people utilise drumming in corporate development to promote connection and to celebrate achievement, the Rhythm2Recovery model, and its combination of rhythm with reflection, allows for a more nuanced examination of the many different issues that impact workplace performance.

The session cards that make up the 'Families, Teams and Communities' package have been developed with organisational development in mind and can be readily tailored to the needs of a business. Themes within this pack include leadership, power dynamics, communication, dealing with change, teamwork, vision and creativity, among others. The use of the drum-circle as a platform for learning in organisational development takes staff out of their comfort zone, away from their traditional sources of power and influence and onto a level playing field. This same experience also replicates the unsettling issue of 'organisational change'; the concept of how people respond to or manage change can be observed and explored through the way different participants respond to being placed into the relatively unknown world of the music-circle.

Communication is also a central issue in effective corporate management and is often at the heart of organisational inefficiencies. Like individuals, families and teams, an organisation can fall victim to unproductive routines or rhythms, and comments such as 'we've always done it this way', 'why change it if it isn't broken?' are often heard in defence of systems and policies that are no longer productive. The Rhythm2Recovery communication exercises, including call and response routines, are particularly useful for exploring patterns of communication that are failing due to their complexity and the many different corporate levels they must transverse. These exercises use music as a language to showcase the importance of simplicity, repetition and clarity in effective communication, as well as addressing listening skills and the importance of timing.

Values, another central tenant of the Rhythm2Recovery model, are also often implicated in toxic workplace environments where individual workers feel disassociated from management, or management teams have become dysfunctional. The increased requirements of corporate governance, and accountability, particularly in regard to risk management, have added layers of generally unproductive and repetitive paperwork to the average worker's job – in fact it is estimated that most employees now spend less than 45 per cent of their time engaged in their core work. To handle this increased level of governance, management has often grown disproportionally in relation to other workplace sectors, which carries the attendant risk of losing touch with those on the ground. I have seen this first hand, turning client-centred, non-government service agencies into corporate-led, profit-driven behemoths that quickly lose direction and their key personnel. This disconnect can often be exposed by exploring values and in particular in examining discrepancies between corporate and personal values using the Rhythm2Recovery values exercises.

A final theme that commonly arises in corporate development work is about the transition of an organisation and its staff through change – 'change management'. Change is a featured topic in the Rhythm2Recovery Families, Teams and Communities syllabus and a relevant subject for many people who are living in this time of unprecedented development, which infers a degree of instability. Too much change is associated with stress and anxiety, whilst many corporate managers recognise the dangers of not changing – not keeping up with changing times, needs, demands, etc. Using the musical exercises and analogies in the Rhythm2Recovery format has been particularly useful in exposing the challenges of adapting to change and the importance of how change is communicated from management down.

Many other central corporate development issues can be examined and addressed using the metaphoric concepts embedded in the Rhythm2Recovery model. Some of the key issues relevant to effective corporate presentations include:

- a professional attitude that includes doing prior research, timeliness, using appropriate language and dressing appropriately

- research being completed prior to the session to understand the key issues to be targeted by the program, and the course structure being aligned to this

- an understanding of key business terminology and commonly used acronyms or abbreviations

- ensuring the appropriateness of the venue – many corporate offices remain unsuitable for these types of programs due to the impact of the sound on other workers, difficult access for equipment and poor acoustics

- encouraging participation and safe disclosures through the support of upper management

- an early focus on examining the alignment between company and personal values

- tying in specific work-related experiences of an organisation's staff to the discussions of the program themes

- the provision of evaluative measures to record perceptions on the worth of the intervention by participants, and their delivery to the contractor prior to invoicing.

5

LESS TALK AND MORE RHYTHM

OPTIONS FOR THE NON-VERBAL

My early work with the mediums of rhythmic music and movement came in response to issues I faced with individuals who lacked confidence in the English language (usually their second or third language). These same individuals found disclosing their thoughts and feelings to a stranger shameful, and many were essentially non-verbal due to a range of presenting conditions, including autism, trauma and cognitive impairment. Beyond this group though, there are still many articulate people whom I work with, who experience the majority of their therapeutic growth through the experiential side of our work together and prefer this side of the program to the reflective dialogue we encourage. In the client-informed feedback I receive, there is a definite preference amongst the majority of those I hear back from for less talk and more rhythm!

One thing about words is that we know they are open to all sorts of misunderstanding, and they can actively work against us by rekindling unhelpful thoughts and emotions or by provoking aggression, blame and resentment. For these and other reasons, my own practice purposefully minimises the use of language in the early sessions, unless I am conscious of an individual's comfort with this medium. I use language to check in with an individual to ensure that they are comfortable, secure, etc., as well as to clarify or summarise a learning point. However, I generally wait for the individual to discuss an issue before expanding upon it verbally. Surprisingly though, for many of the individuals who present with a history of resistance to therapy and non-verbal behaviour, the rhythmic music we engage in loosens their tongues and they often become enthusiastic verbal responders.

For individuals and groups who for various reasons are unable to work through language, many of the musical activities attached to this model can be delivered with positive outcomes using body language cues for instruction instead of verbal directions. There are many specialist practitioners, including music therapists and speech therapists, working with music to assist non-verbal populations to develop language skills, and this work has been particularly effective in assisting the enhancement individuals' speech rate, pitch, variability and intelligibility (Tamplin, 2008). However, this is a specialised realm and not the aim of this resource. The Rhythm2Recovery model is primarily aimed at social and emotional development, and the fact that much of this type of learning comes through the social interaction necessitated by the experiential nature of the exercises themselves means that non-verbal participants can still benefit significantly from their involvement.

Say it Through Your Drum

Use the following techniques to assist people to answer questions through their drums:

- Ask people to answer using a rumble – 'Answer with a rumble if you…'

- Ask people to use one Bass note to answer 'Yes' – 'If you agree with this, play one Bass note.'

- Ask people to use two Bass notes to answer 'No' – 'If you disagree with this, play two Bass notes.'

- Ask people to use three Bass notes to answer 'Not sure' – 'If you are unsure, play three Bass notes.'

Note: The use of the 'Rumble if' as a questioning technique in this manual is adapted from an exercise first shown to me by Arthur Hull.

Much speech leads inevitably to silence
Better to hold fast to the void

Lao Tzu,
Tao te Ching

6

COUNSELLING AND FACILITATION SKILLS

6.1 Core Skills

This model is for professionals working predominantly with individuals and groups of people who face personal difficulties and require support in managing many of life's daily challenges. It is presumed that professionals working with these populations have undertaken appropriate study to carry out their practice ethically, appropriately and effectively. However, one of the keys to best practice in the counselling professions is ongoing, reflective practice (Miller, 2010). So this section provides a brief review of the core skills required to deliver the Rhythm2Recovery model effectively in order to improve the daily lives of those individuals we seek to support.

6.1.1 Building Trust and Rapport

Evidence on effective treatment and effective psycho-social education is clear that a key determinant is the ability of the practitioner to build a trusting and engaging alliance with the individual or group they are working with (Norcross, 2009); effectiveness being described as sustained improvements in the quality of individual lives. Known by a number of terms, the therapeutic alliance or therapeutic relationship is predicated on a trusting and respectful connection. The music components of Rhythm2Recovery interventions are one of the primary tools for building this type of relationship, as music is a medium that unites people emotionally. However, many people have fears associated with learning or performing music, and thus the method of introduction to playing a drum or percussion instrument must be safe and successful.

Developing a trusting relationship is not easy when individuals have histories of betrayal or insecure attachment, and many different, sometimes unavoidable, elements can enter the relationship and sever or disrupt this connection. It is important that counsellors or facilitators are patient and don't set their expectations too high too soon and that there is an acceptance that sometimes the relationship will not gel. One of the key reasons it is recommended to have a co-facilitator in group work is for this very reason – unpredictable factors stemming from an individual's past may see them reject the support of one facilitator yet enable them to bond in a supportive manner with another.

What we do know in terms of how to strengthen the therapeutic bond is that positivity, warmth and a supportive, empathetic and non-judgmental approach is critical and that the process needs to be collaborative and empowering. A key point in the way the quality of a therapeutic alliance transfers to improved developmental outcomes relies not just on this bond, but also on the way in which the individual and practitioner work together to clarify the goals of the intervention and the methods used (Norcross, 2009). The Rhythm2Recovery model is an empowering, strength-based approach that replicates many of the principles of PP and focuses on positivity, strengths, resourcefulness and hope. A collaborative process allows the participants direct input into the therapeutic process itself, determining the themes of focus, actively participating in the exercises, contributing to discussions and providing feedback on the process and how it may be improved in order to achieve mutually agreed-upon goals.

CONNECTING THROUGH RHYTHM
Age range: 5 years and up

With people who may be anxious, it can be useful to start an individual counselling session, using the drum as a vehicle for building safety, trust and connection. The counsellor sits side on to the individual they are supporting and invites them to play the drum as a fun opening to their work together: 'I'll play something and you join in by either copying me or finding your own rhythm – something that connects to mine.'

It is important to start with a very simple pattern and to avoid too much direct eye contact at this stage – just focusing on the drum.

This routine can become a safe way of starting each session and also be used to explore issues of social connection: 'What are we doing that allows our rhythms to connect like this and how might we use these skills to improve our connection with others generally?

6.1.2 Expressing and Validating Feelings

Emotional reactivity or poor regulation is one of the universal features of socially isolated individuals who exhibit anti-social or problem behaviours. Much of the work on emotional regulation starts with emotional awareness, and the Rhythm2Recovery resource contains a number of exercises to assist participants to express and identify their feelings (Section 16.1 'Additional Exercises for Emotional Awareness'). Across all our work with the drum, we encourage individuals to express their feelings and emotions safely, through the instrument itself: for example, 'Play how that felt on your drum.' And we extend that practice into identifying and naming those responses: for example, 'Can you put a name or names to that feeling?' – sometimes multiple feelings arise from the same incident.

Validating feelings is acknowledging that all of us have little control of what feelings surface in response to different circumstances, and as such our individual feelings are both real and reasonable. Validation is a form of acceptance and builds emotional security whilst fostering a deeper empathetic connection. It allows people to feel understood, which in turn opens doors to further assistance. Validation can also be a useful means of helping an individual reflect on the nature and source of their feelings. Validating feelings does not mean accepting the expression of those same feelings when these are done in ways that hurt oneself or others.

It is not always easy to validate another's feelings, particularly when they are critically directed at you. Validating an individual's negative feelings towards you is a way of acknowledging a breakdown in your communication with them – the impact of your intention caused feelings you were not predicting. Breakdowns in communication are common when working with language and individuals who are often overly sensitive to criticism. Validating another's critical feelings towards you, as a practitioner, necessarily means avoiding defensiveness or explaining yourself and instead focusing on acknowledging the authenticity of their response.

6.1.3. Active Listening and Responding

Much has been written about the importance of active or reflective listening in counselling and group facilitation, yet it remains one of the least developed skills in the therapeutic toolbox. Every month I work with professional counsellors and educators on effective practice, and as part of this session run through a simple training drill on listening (see 12.6.2 'Communication'). Each time, the vast majority – paid professionals who are trained to listen well – flunk the test. Why is good listening so hard and how can we improve our skills in this area? Part of the problem is that there is little formal training in listening and to improve our skills requires time, motivation and self-discipline – we have to do it (practise) ourselves. Another barrier is the body's constant filtering process (estimated at processing 400 billion bits of data per second), which blocks out unnecessary sound in order to allow us to focus on what is important to us at any given time. Although this generally serves us well, it may also reduce our capacity for deeper reflective listening and staying attuned to the person we are listening to (Wolvin and Coakley, 1995).

The key to effective listening is attention – an active psychological process unrelated to hearing, which is a passive physiological process – not just to what is being said, but also to the communication cues of tone, speed and pitch and the presenting body language. Listening effectively means understanding, and requires the receiver to seek clarification and to verify their understanding by responding. Active listening is showing genuine interest in what is being said and ensures the person talking feels understood, respected and appreciated, which in turn encourages openness and honesty. These skills are enhanced by practice and a focused awareness of the many internal and external barriers to deeper listening. Barriers include the habit of simultaneously formulating a response to a person whilst they are speaking and competing stimuli such as background noise, intruding thoughts and anxieties, and physiological needs such as hunger, as well as our own judgments and biases and the complexity of the message itself.

Mindfulness practice is a key exercise for increasing our listening capacity, helping us maintain focus whilst simultaneously avoiding the wayward journey of our distracting thoughts. Mindful listening is that which involves no judgment nor a pressing need to respond. Practising mindful listening – giving our full attention, both of the internal and external experience, to the listening process – allows us to attune to others and offer a deeper level of care and support. 'Mindful Awareness Script – Sound' 12.2.2(b) can be used to further this skill.

6.1.4 Encouraging Reflection and Broadening Perspective

A core part of the Rhythm2Recovery model is extending an individual's understanding of the issues addressed by the rhythmic activities through pairing these with cognitive reflection via discussion. For certain populations this will be impractical and the outcomes of the intervention will be drawn solely from non-verbal musical and movement activities. However, for most people, combining the music with cognitive reflection delivers a broader therapeutic process that increases the opportunity for positive outcomes, growth and understanding.

Facilitating dialogue is another skill that rests upon creating a safe context. A reluctance by participants to voice their opinions, thoughts and feelings is generally predicated on a history of shame, where their contributions may have previously been derided or ridiculed. This danger is higher in group therapy, where it is important to have strict boundaries around the way people respond to each other and to monitor conversations to ensure disagreements are handled respectfully. I have found using the drum to help people respond to and answer questions is helpful in the early stages of our relationship, before moving on to verbal contributions as their confidence grows. The use of the drum raises energy levels and avoids the gaping silence that often accompanies questions that focus attention on an individual and may cause shame or embarrassment.

The Speaker's Chair
An Exercise for building trust

One key exercise for involving participants in reflection is 'The Speaker's Chair'. This exercise is based on the 'musical chairs' format, where the rhythm is halted for a set number of beats while everyone moves places in the circle. In the 'Speaker's Chair' exercise, a chair is identified as the one from which an individual speaks or answers the question. The facilitator counts down the rhythm to a stop (4, 3, 2, 1, STOP) and then each person moves one place anti-clockwise – whoever moves into the speaker's chair answers the question on the topic under discussion before counting the rest of the group, back into the rhythm (1, 2, Let's all play).

In the individual session cards accompanying this book, there are a number of questions to help begin a discussion. These questions are a starting point only, and being predominantly 'open ended' provide a gateway to further conversation as the facilitator responds to the answers provided. The skilled practitioner uses the responses to these initial questions to extend the discussion in the direction of most relevance to the individual or group – areas of relevance are thus determined and highlighted by the participants themselves through the subjective nature of their contribution. As in cognitive behavioural therapy, the practitioner is alert to faulty or unhelpful reasoning that leads to maladaptive behaviour. In response to these types of beliefs – for example black and white thinking, generalisations, tunnel vision, negativity, self-blame or labelling – the practitioner offers relevant examples showcasing different perspectives that force a re-evaluation of the issue without coercion or shame.

Other avenues for increasing the level of participation in the discussions in group situations are to have people working together in pairs to provide joint responses and to develop an expectation from early on that everyone will contribute (to a scale of their choice) but that passing is not encouraged. Although this is contradictory to the concept of autonomy for the individual participant, it can be introduced in a way that is not over-demanding – for example, a response may be one strike on your drum. The problem with 'passing' in group discussions, particularly with young people, is that it is an easy way out and can easily become infectious, leading to the whole group abstaining from the discussion.

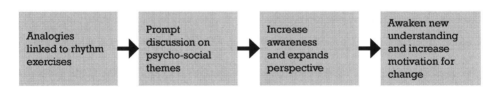

6.1.5 Summarising

Summarising is the skill of taking the main points from a discussion and condensing these into a short statement that helps clarify an individual or group understanding of an issue. It is closely related to the skill of paraphrasing, which is used on a smaller scale and involves a more literal reinterpretation of another person's statement. Both these practices are aimed at helping individuals clarify their thoughts, feelings and ideas, and communicate a level of understanding between the practitioner and those they are supporting. Summarising often occurs immediately prior to the end of a session (or program) in order to refocus on the key issues under consideration, what has been achieved together during the course of the session or program and what the expectations of both parties are in terms of future action.

Summarising is particularly important in group discussions where contributions by different group members may lead to a wide range of perspectives and ideas being considered within a discussion. In these situations, participants can be left confused about the nature of the issue under review unless the facilitator is able to draw out the main points and clarify these in a summary. When disparate points of view are raised in discussions, I generally look to reinforce common themes or uniting factors but sometimes have to make the point that 'people do have different experiences and perspectives on these issues and each person has to find a position that sits comfortably with them and their own values'.

6.2 Cultural Awareness

In today's multicultural world, it is important that counsellors and facilitators are alert to cultural sensitivities and are able to create an environment of cultural security that allows for active and equal participation for people of all cultural backgrounds. Thankfully, music has always been a bridge between people, circumventing manmade boundaries and prejudices. Cultural sensitivity is even more important when the practitioner and individual/s are from different cultural backgrounds. A range of common myths and misconceptions exist with regard to different cultures and there is an ethical responsibility on the part of any practitioner to familiarise themselves with the socio-political factors that affect minorities. It is also critical to recognise the different world views that may influence the relationship between a helper and an individual and their effectiveness in perceiving and interpreting individuals' needs (Sumari and Jalal, 2008). In my work with Aboriginal people across Australia and North America, asking permission and seeking clarification from local people (including cultural leaders or elders) has been critical in avoiding the pitfalls of cultural misunderstanding and promoting a trusting and respectful working partnership.

Music has a special significance in cultures across the world, with different traditions, protocols and prohibitions that govern the way it is expressed. Drumming in particular cultures is an art form closely tied to cultural identity, and its misuse can be seen as disrespectful. The concept of cultural appropriation – taking elements of another culture without permission – also lies close to the surface in relation to the growing use of drumming in Western society, due to the ongoing exploitation indigenous peoples have faced since first contact; thus there remain strong sensitivities to these issues. As a mark of respect, the Rhythm2Recovery model does not utilise traditional cultural rhythms and refrains where possible from using traditional cultural instruments. People who have obtained the cultural authority to use traditional drumming may do so, but I would still always recommend asking advice and permission from cultural elders as an added precaution in order to remove doubt and avoid trespassing in this area.

6.3 Managing Difficult Behaviours

Challenging behaviours are part and parcel of working with 'high-risk' populations, including individuals with low levels of emotional control and behavioural problems. Central to reducing the regularity and intensity of these occurrences are the skills of the practitioner in establishing a safe environment and a trusting therapeutic relationship, as well as the way they respond to, and manage, these situations when they do arise. There are a range of preventative strategies that should always be considered prior to any sessional work and these include:

- accessing up-to-date background information that may have relevance to an individual's emotional state

- having a safety plan for individuals with a history of violent or aggressive behaviours

- having access to collegial support

- implementing a pre-assessment process for group membership that evaluates an individual's readiness for group work

- separating individuals whose defiant behaviours are likely to reinforce one another

- setting and maintaining boundaries – working with individuals to establish boundaries that ensure emotional and physical safety

- reducing arousal levels by utilising a neutral learning space free from other stimuli and talking and playing music at low volume and slower tempos. (Note: High-energy drumming can be damaging in the wrong situation.)

Challenging behaviour is a form of communication, provoked by specific stimuli and generally governed by the consequences of what follows. These behaviours are purpose driven and often connected to an unfulfilled need to obtain something (e.g. attention, peer-prestige or power) or to escape something (e.g. bullying, shame or boredom) (Carr *et al.*, 2002). Being able to recognise what is driving the behaviour is the first step in being able to negate it. In order to implement appropriate consequences or strategies, the facilitator has to remain objective, avoid personalising the dispute and not react emotionally. Easier said than done!

6.3.1 Safety

As previously mentioned, a large number of behavioural issues can be avoided by focusing on establishing a safe and secure environment for participants. For many people safety relates closely to stability and consistency; thus predictable routines, faces, spaces and the environment itself can help reduce anxieties and defensiveness born from uncertainty. Closed groups, where membership stays the same each session, are always preferable, as new faces mean levels of trust must be re-established. Equally, changing facilitators or having new staff members sit in on sessions can undermine safety for participants and impact behaviour. Safety is also critical in group work practice where individuals with social phobias can become very uncomfortable and where power dynamics can leave individuals vulnerable to bullying or physical violence. My work in prisons has been a salutary lesson in the challenges of group make up, where putting the wrong associates together can quickly lead to unresolvable conflict. Pre-assessment for entry into group programs is critical if groups are to be successful.

6.3.2 Avoiding Reacting and Finding the Right Response

Probably the most common inflammatory actions in response to challenging behaviours are those that are emotionally reactive. At some stage or another every practitioner will encounter an individual who gets under their skin and provokes a negative emotional reaction. Learning how to distance and calm yourself in these situations is critical if you are to avoid inflaming a conflict situation.

These are often the same skills we teach in social and emotional learning programs and include breathing strategies, time out, acknowledging your feelings through 'I statements' and handing over the response to another colleague whilst you restore your equilibrium. Young people in particular have a heightened awareness of an adult's emotional state and are strongly impacted by their negative emotions. This can lead to a potentially disastrous cycle where their behaviour triggers a stressful reaction from the facilitator, reinitiating and reinforcing the same causal behaviour (Yoon, 2002).

Responding to challenging behaviours must be done in ways that reduce the intensity of the incident, not inflame it. In a power struggle between an individual and a practitioner the aim is not to assert control (win) but to move through the incident quickly and get back to the helping relationship with egos intact. Power struggles can generally be defused by treating people well, validating feelings, providing choices, giving room to settle emotions and disengagement. The quicker you can disengage, the quicker the negative energy loses its focus.

Disarm
An Exercise for Understanding Power Struggles

Examine the phrase 'It takes two to tango' in relation to conflict.

Ask the individual you are working with to put their hand against yours, or in groups ask people to pair up and to place their hand against their partner's, palm to palm at shoulder height – then ask them to push very gently with their hand.

Stop the group and explore the response – when you push, most will push back. How does this relate to conflict generally?

Now in each pair determine who will push and who will not. Each pair should place their hands together again and this time when the assigned person pushes, the other person is to pull their hand away.

Discuss the concept of disarming anger by withdrawing from conflict using this example.

What happens when one person decides to withdraw from the power struggle? How hard do you find it to withdraw? Who wins when someone decides to withdraw? Who is the one exercising power when someone decides to withdraw?

Note: This is based on the soft martial arts principle of going with or bypassing another's energy rather than working against it.

Given the authoritative power of a practitioner, modelling is also a critical part of any behavioural management strategy. The practitioner's skill at negotiating conflict provides a useful lesson for the observer as to how such incidents are managed and a key learning opportunity for teaching alternatives to aggression and problem solving generally. In group situations it can also be highly effective and empowering to defer this process to the group as a whole, rather than take sole responsibility when problem behaviours impact the session. The group takes responsibility for managing the issue (avoiding blame and focusing on the issue, not on an individual) and learns conflict resolution skills at the same time.

The exercise 'Rumble in the Jungle' 16.4. (e) can also be a useful one to explore conflict.

6.3.3 Setting and Maintaining Boundaries

Boundaries are a critical element of safety for both the practitioner and the individual. Boundaries are also an essential element of healthy relationships and appropriate social interaction, and thus their inclusion and examination can be useful in multiple ways. In one-to-one therapeutic work, discussing boundaries around your working relationship early in the first session can help to avoid misconceptions about your role and ensure ethical issues arising during your time together are handled appropriately. It can also serve as a gateway for the discussion of boundaries generally and how they are impacting other relationships in the individual's life.

In group work the drawing up of group 'rules or guidelines' is common practice and generally also occurs in the first session. Rules can sometimes be seen as punitive and it can be useful to focus on what needs to occur, rather than what shouldn't occur. It is important that this is an inclusive process, so that all have ownership of any agreed constraints and the purpose of establishing these markers of behaviour are clear – Why have boundaries? What purpose do they serve? Again, this process provides a ready segue into more personal discussions on the role of boundaries in relationships generally. The exercise 'Hands Off!' 12.1.5(a) has been designed as a fun way of exploring boundaries and can be used to help draw up behavioural guidelines for a group program.

Boundaries are also closely related to our values – what we care about – and this relationship is a critical one to draw attention to; we protect and stand up for the things we value. Without a clear sense of our values, we lose that guiding principle and with it the security and confidence that comes from knowing what we stand for (identity) and having clear boundaries in place. Once established, values serve as a guide for behaviour across the life span.

6.3.4. Maintaining Momentum and Flow

In my own practice one of the keys areas I focus on, in order to minimise behavioural problems and maximise engagement and sessional outcomes, is momentum – maintaining and sustaining flow throughout the session. This momentum is about progressing smoothly between activities, avoiding dead spots and stark transitions and not over-exposing or satiating individuals with too much of one activity or topic (Kounin, 1971). Individuals and counsellors often emerge at the end of a Rhythm2Recovery session with the statement 'I can't believe that time went so fast', verbalising the feeling that no time at all had passed as they found themselves immersed in the 'flow' of musical activity and constantly focused and engaged.

At the heart of this experience is the practitioner's ability to monitor the individual or participants they are working with and call upon a range of activities to implement in response to their needs. Physical activity is also important to avoid the restlessness that often accompanies prolonged discussions. Most experts agree that sustained attention is generally exhausted at around the five-minute mark (Medina, 2008), so moving between activities every five minutes is a useful marker; and since attention increases significantly when we are interested in what is going on, ensuring participants have input into sessional content, maintaining variety, recognising achievement and encouraging active participation are all useful ways of maintaining interest.

Musical activities, and in particular rhythmic drumming, have great potential to absorb people into a state of flow, where they lose track of time and become completely immersed in the activity itself. Within this state people lose their self-consciousness and are rewarded with feelings of serenity and mastery. In therapeutic and educational situations, this state leads to high levels of focus and improved performance and skill development, whilst simultaneously reducing boredom and anxiety (Csikszentmihalyi, 1997). It also allows the practitioner to observe more natural behaviours as opposed to the often contrived behaviour displayed in therapy situations where individuals may be highly self-conscious and sometimes purposefully deceitful or misleading.

6.3.5 Encouraging Responsibility and Avoiding Blame

In order to take control of your life, you have to accept a level of responsibility for your actions. For many people who are struggling with maintaining control over their lives and who often have personality difficulties that undermine their ability to form healthy relationships with others, blame and a lack of responsibility is common. When we blame others for our situation, we automatically hand them control of our lives and give away our autonomy. Learning to swap blame for responsibility (towards self and others) is a critical step in regaining control of your life and healing your relationships. Blame is also at the heart of much inter-personal conflict and can quickly undo the group process. Establishing boundaries around the use of blame can help people learn how to resolve conflict without putting others down and avoids the defensiveness, resentment and aggression that blame engenders. See 'The Blame Game' 12.3.10(b) exercise.

6.3.6 Avoiding Expert Status and Competition

One of the barriers to the development of a good relationship between a practitioner and the people they work with, and a common element in the undermining of Rhythm2Recovery interventions, is the differentiation that occurs when the practitioner is portrayed as the expert and the individual receiving support is portrayed as needy. These perceptions are often reinforced by the expectations and behaviour of both parties and serve to isolate each from the other. In ACT there is a useful metaphor that ideally describes both parties as mountaineers climbing adjacent peaks, each with their own mountain to climb, but with the practitioner high enough to be able to see across to the individual's peak and make out some of the obstacles and opportunities that the individual may not be able to see for themselves. This parable acknowledges that nobody is an expert when it comes to other people's lives and that we are all finding our way, and through working together we can assist each other in making the climb easier and more enjoyable (Hayes, Strosahl and Wilson, 1999).

Many people who enter Rhythm2Recovery programs come with a poor self-concept and a 'I'm bound to fail' mentality. The idea of playing music, something untried and thus unpredictable, often heightens those thought processes and the fears associated with them. For the practitioner, introducing the musical elements

of the program in an achievable way is critical, and that usually means slowly, repetitively and simply. One of the biggest obstacles to an individual's confidence in this area (initiation into playing music) is for the practitioner to showcase complex drumming skills (or show off!). When an individual with little confidence sees a practitioner exhibiting a high level of skill on the

instrument, it can exacerbate their defeatist attitude – 'I'll never play like that, why should I bother with this', or raise their anxiety – 'Am I going to have to play like that, impossible – I'll make a fool of myself'. High-level drumming skills are not a requirement of these interventions and unless checked can be destructive to the therapeutic alliance.

6.3.7 Empowerment

A critical focus for any practitioner working in support of another human being is ensuring their services enable and strengthen the capacity of those they are working with. There is a very real danger for many of us in the human services field, that our work may undermine this principal and leave those we work with more dependent, particularly when our clients are seeking answers and hold us in high regard. Christopher Small (1977) recognised this same danger in our relationship to music generally when he wrote: 'Music is too important to be left to the musicians, and in recognizing this fact we strike a blow at the experts' domination, not only of our music, but also of our very lives. If it is possible to control our own musical destiny, provide our own music rather than leaving it altogether to someone else to provide, then perhaps some of the other outside expertise that controls our lives can be brought under control also.' In Rhythm2Recovery the practitioner must work consciously to ensure that power dynamic does not seep into their practice and that, as in the ACT model, they avoid expert status and are instead, fellow journeymen on the road to self discovery.

7

DRUM-CIRCLE FACILITATION SKILLS

In the Rhythm2Recovery model we facilitate from a sitting position in the circle, as an equal member of the group. This reduces the power differential that occurs when a leader stands and directs from a raised position, or in the centre of the circle, and in so doing separates themselves from those they are working with. There are considerable dangers in the practitioner taking on a dominant leadership role in the group process, or even in individual therapy situations, and there are many subtle influences that can shift the relationship in that direction, including transference. To balance this risk, there needs to be a constant focus on empowering the individual or participants and supporting them to lead and initiate actions and ideas, as well as to accept responsibility, both in the discussions and in the musical parts of the program, whenever possible. It is particularly important to encourage this inclusive and equitable process from the beginning of any contact.

Facilitation from a sitting position still utilises a range of skills and protocols developed over the years by practice leaders in the community drum-circle movement. This section details some of the essential elements of effective drum-circle facilitation.

- Clarity – Any instruction to the group needs to be clear and concise – keep you instructions short and simple and wherever possible utilise hand signals instead of language. Always lower the volume of the group prior to giving verbal instruction.

- Positivity – Enter the process with a positive and encouraging spirit. Feelings are infectious and your enthusiasm, positivity and encouragement will resonate with others and increase their motivation and levels of enjoyment. Remember to smile!

- Genuineness – Be yourself – be confident in your role, who you are and what you are offering to the group. Find your own style – one that sits comfortably with you and allows you to relax.

- Have fun – Don't take it all too seriously. When things go wrong, that's a learning opportunity. Be prepared to laugh at yourself and share the laughter with others.

7.1 Signalling (as pioneered by A. Hull)

There are a number of universal hand and body movements that can be utilised in the drum-circle to facilitate music making by the group without relying on language. The following are some of the more common ones used in Rhythm2Recovery sessions:

- Getting Everyone's Attention – This is critical prior to initiating any instruction (verbal or non-verbal). The 'Attention Call' is done by making eye contact with each person individually whilst raising one hand above your head and pointing skyward. No further instruction should be given until you are sure you have everyone's attention.

- Marking the Pulse – Sometimes people lose their way in the rhythm, especially when more complex rhythms surface or parts speed up. The facilitator can assist with this by marking the pulse (the first note of the bar) with their feet (an exaggerated stomp) or with their hands (up and down rhythmic movement similar to conducting tempo). Other less common ways of reinforcing and stabilising tempo are to use a bell or through body movement.

- Stopping the Group – A horizontal slice of the air (stop cut) with the extended arm/s and hand/s (stop cuts can be made with one or two hands) moving across the front of the body in a clear cutting motion on time with the beat (usually on the first note of the bar).

- Continue to Play – Extending the arm in the direction of those (individuals or subgroups) who you wish to keep playing and rotating the wrist outwards from the body. I usually reinforce this movement with the words 'Don't stop' and 'Keep going'.

- Counting Down to STOP – Holding the hand out with four fingers raised and thumb hidden and reducing the number of fingers in time with the beat: 4 – 3 – 2 – 1, followed by the 'stop cut' (usually on the first note of the bar).

- Back to the Groove – Getting the group to restart after a gap of silence, we voice the words 'One, two, let's all play' or something similar. The numbers and syllables rest on the beats and are timed to restart the group on the first note of the bar.

- Volume Up – The hand is extended horizontally towards the individual, section or whole group with the palm facing up. Increasing the height of the extended arm relays a signal to keep increasing the volume until you stop.

- Volume Down – The hand is extended horizontally towards the individual, section or whole group with the palm facing down. Reducing the height of the extended arm relays a signal to keep decreasing the volume until you stop.

- Sculpting Parts – Selecting a part or parts of a group to differentiate roles. Always remember to ensure some members, or a section of the group, keep playing before sculpting another part of the group to stop playing. Use two vertical hands (arms extended, fingers together) along with individual eye contact to indicate the boundaries of the chosen subgroup and, once identified, ask them to either 'continue to play' (rotating wrist away from the body) or 'stop' (stop cut).

- Getting Faster/Getting Slower – The signal for getting faster or slower varies between facilitators, but I tend to use a scooping action with my cupped hand, with my hand speed marking the changing tempo (as in 'Marking the Pulse'). Be careful with changes of tempo – it is vital to mark the pulse when you have reached the speed you want or else the change will continue unabated into chaos.

- Rumble – Hands out horizontally in front of the body and wrists or fingers flickering up and down (like slapping a drum or playing a piano very fast).

7.2 The Drum-Circle as Ongoing Recreation

Across the world there is a growing community of recreational drum-circles offering thousands of people a weekly opportunity to socialise safely with others and play music together. These gatherings provide the practitioner with an ongoing resource for those individuals they are working with, which is particularly useful when a program concludes. For the many individuals who experience social isolation, or for whom unstructured recreational time is an invitation for trouble, drum-circles offer a rewarding opportunity to congregate with others, develop new relationships and reap the multiple benefits of community music making.

Establishing a recreational drum-circle is also a great option for sustaining the rewards of a rhythm based psychological intervention at its conclusion. At the end of a Rhythm2Recovery program we often work with the host organisation to help set up a weekly drum-circle where people can meet and play rhythmic music in safety. Basic instruction in drum-circle facilitation techniques, including many of those from Section 7.1, can allow the participants themselves to run and manage these events, offering furthering empowerment and autonomy. Sometimes these groups also add a performance element to their repertoire and

 may go on to represent their organisation at different community events. This is particularly powerful when they are taught how to integrate audience participation with their own music making; thus instead of just playing for people, they are truly interacting and sharing, allowing music to break down any barriers of separation or isolation.

To find a local drum-circle near you see www.drumcircles.net/international circlestext.html.

> *Where I come from we say that rhythm is the soul of life, because the whole universe revolves around rhythm, and when we get out of rhythm, that's when we get into trouble.*
>
> *Babatunde Olatunji*

8

THE CONTEXT

This section covers how best to establish the right therapeutic environment for effective practice using the Rhythm2Recovery model. During my time using rhythmic music in therapy I have worked to deliver individual sessions and group programs in a large variety of settings, including prisons, hospitals, schools, detention facilities, psychiatric units, living rooms, community centres, police and citizen clubs, trauma centres, remote communities and the great outdoors. Some of these places have been conducive to learning, whilst many others actively work against it. Often you have little choice of where you will be working but, where possible – by ensuring an appropriate space, you are one step closer to achieving positive outcomes for those you work with. To do this requires the availability of a suitable space in the first place, some pre-planning and the support of a person of influence within the contracting organisation.

8.1 Room Set Up

Rhythm2Recovery programs involve drumming, and in both individual and group settings the sound can become problematic for those working or living nearby. The contractor should provide a space that is separated from other workers or has inbuilt acoustic dampening. Acoustics are important for the participants as well, as a space that has poor acoustics (many gymnasiums, for example) can be aggravating and potentially cause hearing loss. A carpeted room with a high ceiling that is not overly large nor too small but provides instead a sense of balance between the room's capacity and the group's size is ideal. Never rely on being provided with a suitable space on hearsay alone – visit and test the space yourself prior to starting your work there. Comfortable seating is important, with chairs (and instrument sizes) allowing participants to hold and play their instruments comfortably – chairs without arms are best, and avoid chairs on rollers.

In schools, a lot of time can be wasted moving desks and creating the right space each week – try to organise a space that allows you to get started quickly. Setting up a room each week is an invitation for young people to play up and often leads to unhelpful levels of arousal. Rooms that have little in the way of furniture or equipment are best. Many of the people utilising these therapies have low levels of focus and are easily distracted, and those with sensory perception disorders are often over-stimulated by rooms that contain a lot of random objects or that are messy and disorganised. Windows can also be problematic, as inquisitive faces often appear when drumming occurs and these will further distract people. This same issue also makes outdoor programs difficult, as they usually invite multiple distractions (visual and acoustic) and the drums will attract (call to) people from a wide distance.

In group work, the drums are set in one circle for a maximum of around 20 persons – if larger numbers are required, concentric circles work well. The drums are initially placed behind the chairs so that the participants can focus on the theme of the session and review group rules and previous learning before the new session begins.

Group Size	Minimum Dimensions
10	20 square metres
20	50 square metres
30	64 square metres
50	80 square metres

Lighting and other furnishings also make a difference to how comfortable people feel in a particular space. Dark or over-exposed (using unnatural lighting) counselling rooms are off putting, and the imagery displayed on walls needs to be thoughtfully considered in light of the issues and triggers that impact individuals. Natural textures are preferable to artificial ones, and the allowance for personal space should ensure that adequate room is given for people to feel safe. A whiteboard is useful, as many exercises require the listing of group responses, and writing up rules, rhythms and other pertinent information can be helpful for visual learners.

8.2 A Supportive Environment

The use of rhythmic music as part of therapeutic or educational programs is still in its infancy and still viewed sceptically by many. I have had personal encounters and heard reports from many professionals where I or they have been deliberately undermined by other professionals who fail to understand and value their work. Having an understanding and supportive working environment is critical to any professional's confidence and performance. It is always beneficial to meet with an individual of influence from the contracting service prior to beginning a program to ensure that they are able to provide the support you require to work effectively in this medium. This same individual should also inform all other staff of your work and how it fits in with the aims of the organisation in order to reduce the potential for confusion or resentment.

Providing staff with an explanatory session prior to beginning your work can also be useful in avoiding this pitfall. Schools and prisons can be particularly difficult environments to work in, where the priority given to your role often falls well down the ladder of the priorities of their management teams. Recently, after several challenging prison programs made much more difficult by staff attitudes, I made sure that prior to a new program being delivered, I would run some officer information sessions – the difference in attitudes and my ease of access was remarkable and made the experience much more valuable for those who participated in it.

8.3 Group Make Up – Pre-Assessment

Groups can quickly become unproductive when people enter with personality disorders or developmental issues that provoke disharmony. Defiant and aggressive personalities can quickly undermine groups by reducing perceived levels of safety, while significant variations in developmental capacity between group members can heighten levels of frustration. It is never wise to allow open access to group work without some pre-assessment and it often takes courage for a facilitator to stand up to an employer or contractor and insist upon a degree of discretion in choosing those suitable for participation.

For youth groups this becomes even more important, as the influence of peers is heightened, and putting too many young people together who present with similar problems can easily reinforce unhealthy behaviours due to the need for social acceptance. This is also a common issue in juvenile detention and drug and alcohol rehabilitation, where people present with common issues and unhealthy behaviour risks become further ingrained. In situations like these, pre-assessment can make a huge difference, allowing for a broader mix of individuals within the group who are more likely to work together and benefit from the experience.

Stigma is also a concern for groups that are formed to address a specific issue. Wherever possible, it can be beneficial, given the universal nature of the Rhythm2Recovery themes, for groups to to be representative of a whole population, rather than a challenging subset. Encouraging a broad representation of individuals in group programs also allows individuals to connect with people they would normally not associate with and learn new ways of interpreting and responding to the world around them. When people are asked at the conclusion of a Rhythm2Recovery program 'What did you gain from your experience?', it is common to hear them reply, 'I made a new friend I would normally not have hung around with.'

Some of the Criteria Used in Group Membership Assessment Interviews

- An individual's attitude towards group membership.

- Histories of aggression and violence.

- Developmental capacity – physical and cognitive abilities.

- Gender.

- Age.

- Family feuding – historical animosity between members of certain families.

- Cultural animosities – historical animosity between members of certain cultural groups.

- Gangland animosities – historical animosity between rival gang members.

- Levels of hyperactivity.

- Motivation (stage of recovery).

- Attendance history - level of commitment.

9

RESOURCES

WHAT YOU NEED TO GET GOING

9.1 Drums

Most of the exercises in this manual involve the use of hand-drums, which come in a wide variety of types and sizes. Depending on your situation, you will require a specific collection of drums suitable for your individual practice or group. As someone who does a lot of group work for external organisations, my own preference is for drums that are easy to transport, and the Remo Versa range is ideal; they also come with specially designed heads for low-impact sound. Specially designed stands are available for the 'Versa range' and some other drums to hold them stably off the ground, which is very useful for people of lower muscle strength. However, if you already have access to Djembes, Bongos, Congas or Frame drums (the most common types of hand-drums) you can readily utilise these in most situations.

For individual work, two equally matched drums are required plus one larger Bass drum (a floor tom from a drum kit can work) that can be played with a mallet. For group work, it is often preferable to have a matching set of drums in order to avoid disputes caused by individual preferences for one type or sized drum over another. Much energy can be wasted, particularly in youth groups, over disputes about who will play which drum.

For older individuals with postural difficulties, and those with disabilities, frame drums and mallets can be beneficial and these are relatively inexpensive.

9.2 Percussion

A number of exercises in this manual utilise percussion instruments, and having a small collection of these instruments – shakers, clave, bells, etc. – can extend your options in the improvised rhythm exercises, add diversity to the group sound and also provide options for those who have problems playing drums. Bells are also good for signalling above the sound of drums and are used for this purpose in many of the exercises. Note: Avoid giving loud bells to individuals with a low sound threshold or poor regulation.

9.3 Tonal Chimes

Tonal chimes (use a pentatonic scale, CDEGA) are made by several suppliers and allow you to quickly and simply bring melody into your rhythmic music with no musical experience necessary. Easy to play and with a pure resonance that creates a calming tranquillity, tonal chimes can readily be used to reinforce the principles of mindfulness through an 'in-the-moment' focus on sound. These instruments combine beautifully with low drums and wooden percussion instruments and can be facilitated using many of the common drum-circle facilitation techniques described in Section 7.1.

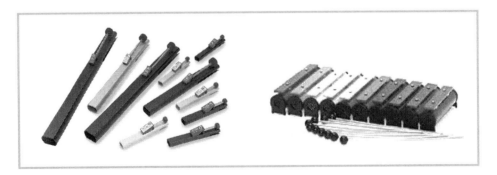

9.4 Recycled Instruments

For those with limited budgets, drums and many different percussions instruments can be made from recycled materials at virtually no cost. Reasonable sounding hand-drums can be made from recycled 15 litre water bottles or other plastic containers and simply decorated with colourful electrical tape or glued-on fabric. Larger Bass drums can be made from plastic garbage cans or larger plastic agricultural drums. Shakers can be made from small containers filled with rice and clave from short offcuts of well-sanded 25 mm hardwood dowel. Making instruments like these together is a great way to start a group rhythm program, and by ensuring people work together in pairs we foster familiarity and cooperation at the same time.

PART 2

GAMES, EXERCISES AND APPLICATIONS

10

A RHYTHM CATALOGUE

This section provides the facilitator with some rhythm songs that have been developed using a scaffolding approach to assist ease of learning. Each part builds upon the successful attainment of the previous part, helping avoid the loss of confidence that comes when expectations exceed capacity, which can reawaken deeply held, inner beliefs of failure. The rhythms here are used as 'seeds' to grow rhythmic confidence in a progressive manner that leads ultimately to the freedom of full improvisation, where the participant is empowered to find their own rhythmic expression, albeit one that connects to the group as a whole.

Sometimes, individuals are able to go straight into playing improvised rhythmic music, and very occasionally people will resent being asked to play set parts, finding them too constraining. However, for most people, moving straight to 'make it up for yourself' is anxiety inducing and limits their contribution to one or two rhythms that they find safe, in much the same way that many people fall back on a limited range of, often inappropriate, life patterns, because these are all they know. Initially providing people with a diverse foundation of rhythmic exercises gives them the confidence to move between different rhythms when they reach the improvised exercises of the Rhythm2Recovery model.

The specific parts and songs introduced here are provided as a starting point only and the practitioner can extend these by utilising other rhythms from the many sources available online or from their existing repertoire, if they already have one. Certain elements remain critical, however, in ensuring a successful transition to confident rhythmic engagement; these include avoiding any competitive element (such as insisting on perfecting technique), ensuring the complexity of the rhythms does not exceed the developmental capacity of the participants (thus reducing frustration and avoiding failure) and encouraging people to use these rhythms as a basis from which to experiment ('make these rhythms your own by expanding upon them if you feel confident in doing so').

10.1 Basic Hand-Drum Technique

Hand-drums come in many different forms from many different cultures and thus professional technique varies, but this manual is not really interested in professional standards when it comes to drumming. Our concerns are primarily with good posture and a simple format for getting a clear sound from your instrument.

10.2 Posture

A focus on posture allows us to assist people whose body carries the weight of their pain and who are often disassociated from their physical self. Good posture impacts both physical and emotional health and can act to reinforce positive changes in self-acceptance and general optimism (Brinol and Petty, 2008). Where possible, good posture for playing hand-drums means sitting up straight, with the natural inward curve of the spine – sitting at the front of the chair with the head level and arms relaxed. Bringing yourself forward on the chair allows a space for the drum between your legs, but is unnecessary when playing smaller drums held on the lap or in the hand.

For larger drums, it is important to open the outlet at the bottom for the sound to come out, and thus the drum is angled slightly away from the body and held in place between the thighs with minimal pressure. From adolescence upwards, a drum with a 25–30 cm diameter head standing approximately 60 cm off the ground will be suitable. Smaller-sized drums will work better for younger children. If you find yourself with smaller-sized Djembes, these can be held easily at the right height when the legs are crossed to form a funnel.

10.3 Occupational Health and Safety

Although music, and drumming in particular, is generally regarded as a relatively benign activity, there are a number of health and safety issues that need to be considered. Perhaps the most important consideration is recognising that drumming can be an arousing and stimulating activity and that this attribute can lead to sensory overload for vulnerable people if not checked. Flores (2011), in a study of an intervention using high-energy African drumming with young people with behavioural disorders, noted an increase in children's levels of anxiety.

I learned very quickly, when I first started using the drum in my practice, about the dangers of over-stimulation and, even with that understanding, I have experienced problems of this type when working with particularly sensitive individuals. These included people suffering from recurring psychotic episodes in psychiatric units who were unable to tolerate the drumming, even with headphones, and young people with hyperactivity disorders who often became over-aroused and unmanageable. Soft, slow drumming is always preferable in these interventions, and earplugs or headphones should always be available.

Hygiene should always be front of mind as well, as the instruments pass from one individual to another. Alcohol wipes are useful as sterilising agents between groups – with a quick wipe usually sufficing. Removing hand jewellery is also recommended, as often fingers swell after playing, causing pain, and the sharp edges of rings can damage a drum skin. Finally, be alert to the hearing dangers of drums played in large groups in rooms with poor acoustics. I have monitored the decibel level of drums in counselling rooms that had soundproofing installed and still found that levels exceeded recommended safety levels when more than ten drums were playing simultaneously.

10.4 Bass and Tone

Commonly used hand-drums have two or more readily available notes, known by different names depending on which instrument is being played. In this manual we predominantly rely on two – the deeper note centred in the middle of the drum, known here as the Bass, and the lighter note obtained at the edge of the head where the drum skin meets its shell, known here as the Tone. Depending on the instrument being played and capacity of the participant/s, further sounds may be explored.

To find a resonant Bass note, hit the middle of the drum with a full hand, connecting as much surface as possible and bouncing off instantaneously to release the sound wave. It is important to emphasise relaxing the hand and not holding too much tension in the arm. Most of the energy comes from the wrist unless high volume is required.

To play a clear, open Tone note, strike the edge of the drum with the full length of the fingers, including the ridge of flesh adjoining the palm. Hold the fingers together but avoid undue tension. Practise this on each drum to find a tone you are comfortable with, as each drum has its own sweet spot. Remember to keep the thumb away from the edge of the drum, as this can be painful if it is struck accidentally.

Bass (B) and Tone (O) Practice Drills

Timing	1 + 2 + 3 + 4 +	1 + 2 + 3 + 4 +	1 + 2 + 3 + 4 +	1 + 2 + 3 + 4 +
Exercise 1	B B B B	O O O O	b b b b	o o o o
Hands	R R R R	R R R R	L L L L	L L L L
Exercise 2	B B O O	B B O O	B B O O	B B O O
Hands	R R L L	R R L L	R R L L	R R L L

10.5 The Flam and Slap

The Flam is the accent note in the Rhythm2Recovery model, requiring significantly less effort to master than the traditional Slap sound and being suitable for many of the lower pitched drums used for therapeutic purposes. Occasionally, a higher note is required for accent, dramatic effect or to heighten attention, and the Flam note fills this purpose. The Flam is played in the same region as the Tone, on the edge of the rim, with both hands hitting the skin almost simultaneously. Performing it with fingers apart raises the pitch of this note even higher.

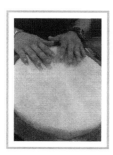

The Slap sound is the most challenging note for the hand drummer – teach the Slap by replicating the Tone technique, but with the fingers apart. The relaxed hand hits the edge of the drum on the pad below the fingers and the separated fingertips ricochet down and touch the skin, creating a bright slapping sound. A Slap played by a professional can sound like a whip cracking!

10.6 Drumming Tablature

B	Bass (centre of drum) beat with right hand
b	Bass (centre of drum) beat with left hand
O	Tone (rim of drum) beat with right hand
o	Tone (rim) beat with left hand
S	Slap beat with right hand: sharp glancing stroke
s	Slap beat with left hand
fl	Almost simultaneous (very slightly offset) rim strike with both hands

Where an individual is left handed, reverse the associations so that the capital letter is played with the left hand and the smaller case is for the right. Avoiding the terms left and right and replacing them with 'Strong' and 'Weaker' hands can help those who have trouble with dyslexia and/or identifying their left and right.

10.7 Not Too Fast!

More than anything else, teaching at too fast a pace undermines the Rhythm2Recovery experience, destroying confidence, increasing anxiety and leading to withdrawal, dejection and defensive behaviours that are often challenging to manage. Be self-aware and also monitor those you work with constantly to ensure people are given a chance to master each rhythm level before increasing tempo or moving to a new rhythm. It is always easy to speed up, but it is much more difficult to renew confidence if you start too fast. I often think about the pace I am planning to begin with and then halve it again before starting.

10.8 Foundation Rhythms

In the Rhythm2Recovery model we use three simple foundation rhythms as the basis for many exercises. As people's capacity increases, these rhythms can be replaced by more challenging parts, but initially these three parts are extremely useful.

Timing	1 + 2 + 3 + 4 +	1 + 2 + 3 + 4 +	1 + 2 + 3 + 4 +	1 + 2 + 3 + 4 +
Foundation 1	B O B O	B O B O	B O B O	B O B O
Foundation 2	B B - -	B B - -	B B - -	B B - -
Foundation 3	B B O O	B B O -	B B O O	B B O -

10.9 Drum Songs

The Heartbeat Rhythms

These are amongst the most widely used universal drumming patterns in the world, and connect intimately with our internal rhythms. Introduce the two Bass notes as the foundation of the rhythm, and the place to return to whenever one gets lost.

Timing	1 + 2 + 3 + 4 +	1 + 2 + 3 + 4 +	1 + 2 + 3 + 4 +	1 + 2 + 3 + 4 +
Part 1	B B - -	B B - -	B B - -	B B - -
Part 2	B B O -	B B O -	B B O -	B B O -
Part 3	B B O O	B B O O	B B O O	B B O O
Part 4	B B OoO	B B OoO	B B OoO	B B OoO
Part 5	B B As many as you like	B B As many as you like	B B As many as you like	B B As many as you like
Part 6	B B With clapping	B B With clapping	B B With clapping	B B With clapping
Part 7	B B With rubbing or scratching	B B With rubbing or scratching	B B With rubbing or scratching	B B With rubbing or scratching
Part 8	B B Add whatever combination you like	B B Add whatever combination you like	B B Add whatever combination you like	B B Add whatever combination you like

Four On the Floor

This rhythm can be used to assist individuals with grounding by slowing the tempo down and emphasising pushing the feet into the floor on the Bass notes.

Timing	1 + 2 + 3 + 4 +	1 + 2 + 3 + 4 +	1 + 2 + 3 + 4 +	1 + 2 + 3 + 4 +
Part 1	B O B O	B O B O	B O B O	B O B O
Part 2	B b O -	B b O -	B b O -	B b O -
Part 3	B o O b	B o O b	B o O b	B o O b
Part 4	O o B -	O o B -	O o B -	O o B -

Feel Your Bass

This rhythm has an earthy feel, which is useful for grounding, and teaches the basic skill of using triplets.

Timing	1 + 2 + 3 + 4 +	1 + 2 + 3 + 4 +	1 + 2 + 3 + 4 +	1 + 2 + 3 + 4 +
Part 1	B b B -	B b B -	B b B -	B b B -
Part 2	O o B o	O o B o	O o B o	O o B o
Part 3	fl B b -	fl B b -	fl B b -	fl B b -
Part 4	O o B b B	O o B b B	O o B b B	O o B b B

One, Two, Three and A Place For Me

This rhythm introduces participants to a three-time pattern, the basis of 6/8 rhythms, and has some some useful hand patterning to improve coordination and motor skills.

Timing	1 + 2 + 3 +	1 + 2 + 3 +	1 + 2 + 3 +	1 + 2 + 3 +
Part 1	B O O	B O O	b o o	b o o
Part 2	B b O	B b O	B b O	B b O
Part 3	O o O B	O o O B	O o O B	O o O B
Part 4	B b O	b B o	B b O	b B o

Swing Time

This rhythm has a swung feel that gives the first note of every bar a little extra length before you bring in the following notes.

Timing	1 + 2 + 3 + 4 +	1 + 2 + 3 + 4 +	1 + 2 + 3 + 4 +	1 + 2 + 3 + 4 +
Part 1	B O o B -	B O o B -	B O o B -	B O o B -
Part 2	B o B o B -	B o B o B -	B o B o B -	B o B o B -
Part 3	fl fl B -	fl fl B -	fl fl B -	fl fl B -
Part 4	B b S b -	B b S b -	B b S b -	B b S b -

11

THE RHYTHMIC WAVE

MINDFULNESS AND EMOTIONAL REGULATION

For a large number of people, the ability to regulate their emotions is an ongoing struggle and overwhelmingly contributes to their inability to negotiate healthy and supportive relationships.

Indeed, most mental suffering is caused by this duopoly (Van Der Kolk, 2014). Emotional regulation is central to wellbeing and positive adjustment. Neurological research has located specific regions of the brain that impact our emotions and the way we respond to them and, critically, many of these areas (comprising the limbic system) are closely impacted by rhythmic music (Levitin, 2009). There is growing evidence to indicate that rhythmic music may positively impact these regions and assist individuals in reducing their vulnerability to the reactivity of those systems when they have become dysfunctional (Chanda and Levitin, 2013).

Certainly, the vast majority of people recognise the impact rhythm and tempo exert on mood; one only has to attend the cinema to see how music impacts our emotions.

The Rhythmic Wave exercise is a core part of the Rhythm2Recovery model and the entry point into the practice of mindfulness. Specific mindfulness scripts accompany many of the session themes and are particularly prevalent in the 'Health and Wellbeing' syllabus. Mindfulness is a core part of the new, third-wave, behavioural therapies and allows individuals to gain renewed awareness and attention on aspects of their world in the present moment. Mindfulness is a technique drawn from religious or spiritual traditions that places the individual as a curious 'observer' of things in the present moment – that is, through mindful practice we are able to consciously notice or pay attention to and observe all elements of our life, internal and external, including our worries and anxieties, without being absorbed by them. We observe our thoughts and feelings instead of getting caught up in them. In therapy this has particular value in assisting people who are preoccupied by worries about the past or future. Mindfulness has great benefits for living generally, allowing people to give greater focus to the world around them and to be more aware in all their actions and behaviours.

For many individuals, being asked to participate in a mindfulness session can be like being asked to do something quite alternative, radical and unpredictable, giving rise to significant apprehension and resistance. Mindfulness is becoming more common, but for many populations the entry into practice is awkward – I have seen classes of school students who spend much of their regular mindfulness class smirking and giggling whilst the facilitator sits 'mindfully' unaware! I also find replacing the word 'mindfulness' with 'focus' – 'we are going to do a focus exercise', helps some populations better understand the process they are entering into. For many 'at-risk' populations the trust required to follow a practitioner through a brief mindfulness exercise is just not there. This is why the Rhythmic Wave exercise was developed. This exercise combines the soothing, grounding pulse of the Bass note with scripts of mindful awareness. In the first session of the Rhythm2Recovery model participants are introduced to the Rhythmic Wave process whereby they move between drumming at relatively high tempo and volume and drumming at slow tempo and low volume (eventually playing just a simple Bass pulse). The transition between the two extremes is gradual, oscillating back and forth, and must be practised several times before eventually becoming routine. This exercise then becomes an ongoing part of each Rhythm2Recovery session to follow.

Once the individual or group have mastered the Rhythmic Wave oscillation technique, the periods of soft, slow drumming become the backdrop to the introduction of mindfulness routines. The single Bass pulse is played on a large Bass drum between 40 and 60 bpm (replicating and inducing alpha brainwaves), and in the initial sessions the practitioner helps the individual focus on aligning their breath to the pulse and maintaining that focus.

Say: 'Relax now, relax your body, loosen any tension and find a comfortable position in your chair – if you prefer to, you may stop drumming.' Pause. 'Focus on and relax any tension in your neck, shoulders, chest, arms, hands, back, hips, thighs, lower legs, feet.' Pause. 'Now turn your focus to your breath – starting

Rhythmic walk   in 3 beats
out 3 beats

with one breath in on a pulse of your choice and releasing that breath some three to four pulses later.' Pause. 'Slowing the breath to the beat of the pulse and focusing on filling the lungs and emptying them slowly and evenly.' Pause. 'Being aware of other thoughts, as they come or go, but always returning to the breath and its alignment to the pulse, grounding you.' Pause. 'Becoming still.' Pause. 'Feeling your breath travelling deep within you.' Pause. 'Breathing slowly and deeply.' Pause. 'Noticing the rise and fall of you diaphragm.' Pause.

This Rhythmic Wave, oscillating between high-energy release and soft, calm reflection, occurs three to five times across the same exercise, with the period spent at the contemplative end (slow and soft) increasing as participants' comfort levels increase. Participants are encouraged to relax their body, close their eyes or focus on one spot as they move into the mindfulness state. Participants may continue to drum, but many stop and leave the drumming to the facilitator. As this process becomes established, new themes can be introduced (see Chapter 12), including observing body sensations or sounds or focusing on specific themes such as love, acceptance or forgiveness.

The Rhythmic Wave exercise assists individuals with emotional regulation issues in three ways. First, the practice of moving between periods of high emotional intensity and a calm state provides a template for de-escalation. The practitioner can use metaphors to clarify this association and nominate, with the individual they are working with, personal stressors that activate the high arousal state and de-stressors to regain a calm state.

Second, the practice of mindfulness allows the individual to separate themselves from the types of thoughts and feelings that are psychologically unhelpful – accepting them, acknowledging them and allowing them to come and go, but at the same time reducing their influence by not being beholden to them.

Third, through the practice of mindful attention we become increasingly alert to our own emotional rhythms and the physical sensations that precede them. We can consciously respond to these, rather than react to them, and avoid unnecessary conflict with others. When we are mindful, we become aware of the way our emotions influence our thoughts and distract us from the present, and we can use this awareness to increase our objectivity.

Teaching mindfulness is a technique that requires some practice in order to get the pace and the tone of the voice right, give clear and concise directions and keep the Bass pulse steady (use a metronome) whilst talking. And remember, no mindfulness script is ever the same twice – the examples here are only there to get you started; make them your own.

11.1. Additional Emotional Regulation Exercises

Almost every activity within the Rhythm2Recovery framework involves a degree of emotional regulation as individuals follow directions or work together with others. However, a number of specific exercises have been developed to assist those for whom this is a dominating concern. Regular use of these exercises, coupled with reflective discussions on the triggers that prompt emotional arousal and strategies to lessen them, can positively impact an individual's level of self-discipline.

(A) THE BODY SCAN

This is a mindfulness technique used to increase our awareness of bodily sensations without judging them. By being aware of how our body manifests our emotions, we gain insight into our feelings and what we are feeling at any given time. This is an essential step towards controlling those feelings whose release would cause us or others to suffer.

Use a simple and very soft Bass pulse (40–60 bpm) or the Rhythmic Wave exercise as the focal point for this awareness exercise. Give instructions in a mellow, clear voice, speaking slowly, in time to the rhythm. Remember, the script below is just a guide – make it your own.

- Relax your body.

- Adjust your body until you feel comfortable and relaxed. You may wish to close your eyes or focus on one spot. Slow your breathing.

- Now focus solely on sounds. Listen to the Bass note of the rhythm first. Listen to it in all its dimensions and let it ground you, centre you and connect you.

- If other thoughts come to mind, acknowledge them briefly and move your focus back to the sound of the Bass note.

- Now move your attention to your feet. Look for any tension, pressure or other sensations. Observe these without trying to change them.

- Breathe gently, slowly.

- Move upwards to your calves, observing; then to your knees and thighs, feeling for any sensations.

- If other thoughts come to mind, acknowledge them briefly and move your focus back to your body.

- Now move upwards to your back, feel for any tension in your back, aching joints, twitches. Then move across to your chest and further on to your shoulders, seeking feelings, sensations, tension or other pressures. Observe rather than try to change anything.

- Stay with your shoulders, a place where many people hold tension. Explore this part of your body, then move slowly up to your neck and look for any feelings of tension there.

- Finally, feel your head. Examine the tension in your jaw and any other areas that might be stiff. Observe without trying to change anything.

- Breathe gently, slowly.

- Now spend some time reviewing your whole body, getting to know your body sensations as an observer, without judgment and with acceptance.

- Slowly come back to a focus on the Bass.

- Hold your focus on the Bass and allow the volume to slowly fade away.

If possible, sit in silence for 40–60 seconds. Alternatively, if you are using the Rhythmic Wave exercise, you can finish by resuming and rebuilding the rhythm again.

(B) HOLD ONTO YOUR RHYTHM

In one-to-one sessions or in groups, an individual must hold their tempo whilst those around them speed up and do their best to bring the individual with them.

(C) PLAY IT FAST, PLAY IT SLOW

In one-to-one sessions or in groups, an individual must gradually reduce the tempo of their rhythm. Everyone starts at a reasonably fast tempo and whilst the rest of the group (or the practitioner) maintains that tempo, the individual must *gradually* reduce their rhythm to a slow and steady beat.

(D) PLAY IT LOUD, PLAY IT SOFT

In one-to-one sessions or in groups, an individual must *gradually* lower the volume of their drumming whilst those around them maintain their louder sound. The individual maintains their soft drumming rather than simply stopping.

Examine these last three exercises in relation to the way people get pulled in (influenced) emotionally by others around them, sometimes into situations that they might be better off avoiding. How can we better resist this pull? How do the emotions of others impact you? Are there people around you who impact your emotions for better or for worse? How do your emotions impact others?

(E) FADE AWAY

This exercise is often used to close a session, with the drumming volume brought down gradually to the point of silence. Prior to starting this exercise, I often ask people if they can try to sit for a few moments with the silence at the end of this exercise.

Note the importance of *gradual* reductions in tempo and sound as an additional measure of control.

FURTHER EXERCISES FOR EMOTIONAL REGULATIONS:

- 'Musical Chairs Version 2' 16.4(d)

- 'Pressure Valve' 12.2.5(b)

- 'The Echo Wave' 12.2.5(d)

- 'Rumble in the Jungle' 16.1.(e)

12

SESSIONAL THEMES AND RHYTHMIC EXERCISES

This section details the exercises found on the 52 sessional rhythm cards that are included as part of this resource pack (see link on p.15). The cards come in five sets of ten, plus one 'Getting Started' card and one 'Finishing Up' card.

The five sets of ten session cards are organised under the following themes:

- Social and Emotional Learning.

- Identity and Culture.

- Strengths and Virtues.

- Health and Wellbeing.

- Families, Teams and Communities.

The cards provide the practitioner with a simple template for a one-hour Rhythm2Recovery session. Each card begins with some details on the session theme and its relevance to individual and community wellbeing, which is used to introduce the subject focus. This is followed by one or more rhythm exercises (details of all exercises below), each of which provides a relevant analogy to help initiate a follow-up discussion – starter questions for this discussion are provided on the card. In most sessions the Rhythmic Wave mindfulness exercise precedes the discussion (see Chapter 11) and provides further consolidation of the issues under review. This is then complemented by another relevant exercise and the session is completed with a period of 'Free Expression', where people are encouraged to release feelings, and the regulatory control exercise 'Fade Away', where the group or individual slowly reduces the volume down to silence.

The templates are flexible, and additional games, drumming exercises, mindfulness practice and discussion can be incorporated where necessary to meet the needs of the participants. At the end of a session, the remaining cards (session themes) of the pack are often displayed to the participants, allowing them to choose which subject area they would like to focus on in the next session, giving the practitioner adequate time to prepare.

The following information will help clarify the purpose of an exercise and who will benefit most from it.

- IND – suitable for individual therapy situations.

- GRP – suitable for group counselling or psycho-social education.

- FAM – suitable for family therapy situations.

- COR – suitable for corporate development work.

- Age range – examples given (note that these exercises are not generally suitable for children below the age of eight, requiring a level of self-reflective awareness and reciprocal relational understanding).

- Key focus areas – examples given.

- Specialist population addressed – examples given.

- See Section 10.6 on rhythm tablature for assistance with understanding the rhythm patterns in this section.

12.1 Getting Started – Introductory Exercises

The exercises in this section are designed for fun and safety. The first session is one where introductions are made, goals are set, boundaries around behaviour are established and expectations are discussed. It is often the first time an individual has played a drum, and this introduction may require particular sensitivity. Rumbles are used to help release nervous tension and to answer questions with safety. The boundary exercise 'Hands Off' and the 'Values' exercises from Section 12.2.1 are often utilised in this session and are useful for establishing a safe framework for working together.

12.1.1 Call and Response Exercises

IND, GRP, FAM, COR. Age Range: All Ages.

Key Focus Areas: Rhythmic confidence, communication, balance.

(A) CALL AND RESPONSE

The facilitator plays a brief rhythm on their drum and the individual or participants echo it back (it is important to keep these rhythms short and simple). As the response becomes more assured, swap roles – again emphasising simplicity. Take it in turns for different people to lead the exercise, and introduce changes in volume.

Variations of this exercise can be done with voice, movement and body percussion.

Use these exercises to explore communication – What makes it work and what gets in the way? What are the key elements of good communication? How does communication impact your relationships currently? How hard is it to listen well? How easy is it to miscommunicate an idea or feeling to someone? What can help us improve our communication skills?

(B) CALL AND RESPONSE OVER A RHYTHM

Have the group play a simple 4/4 foundation rhythm and choose a leader among them to hold it steady. Then choose a select number of participants to stop drumming and instead follow your lead in 'Call and Response', aligning it to the background beat.

Discuss the different roles of the two sides and how these balance each other – with the foundation providing a stable platform as a base for exploration, risk taking and creativity.

(C) CALL AND RESPONSE INTO A RHYTHM (AS TAUGHT BY A. HULL)

Play a range of call and response patterns in 4/4 time and then settle on one simple pattern and repeat this several times. Give a signal to repeat and keep going – using eye contact with the whole group and a rotating hand – then model the same rhythm on your own drum as a continuous rhythm (that is, repeat it steadily) and play as a group.

One at a time, each person in the group can then offer up their own call and repeat it until it becomes a group rhythm. Emphasise simplicity.

12.1.2 Rumble Games

IND, GRP, FAM, COR. Age Range: 8 years and up.

Key Focus Areas: Engagement, universality, communication, emotional expression, teamwork, rhythmic timing and coordination.

Note: 'Rumbles' are an excellent technique for beginning sessions, as a person cannot make a mistake playing a rumble. Rumble games are useful for reducing anxiety and building confidence, as well as for releasing energy and tension.

RUMBLE FACILITATION

Demonstrate a rumble and change between parts of the drum, volume and tempo to explore different effects. Conduct the rumble so that it changes in dynamic. If working in a group, experiment with different parts of the group playing louder and others playing softer and alternating these like a wave. Allow your participants to have a turn at conducting the rumble.

Use this exercise to explore communication and leadership issues, as well as to allow people the chance to release pent-up energy.

(A) PASS THE RUMBLE (USEFUL FOR EMOTIONAL ATTUNEMENT)

Pass a rumble from one person to the other using a range of different communication techniques to do so. Ask participants to find a signal that will tell the other person that they are to take over the rumble – it may be calling that person's name, using eye contact, pointing – get creative! Ask people to accept the rumble from the sender at the same emotional intensity (volume and tempo) and then change it for themselves before passing it on.

Use this exercise to explore the different ways people communicate and what works and what doesn't. Using eye contact can be helpful for individuals with 'gaze aversion' issues, but may also be problematic for people from cultures where eye contact is seen as an aggressive form of communication (e.g. some Australian Aboriginal groups).

(B) RUMBLE BASKETBALL (YOU CAN TRY A RANGE OF SPORTS)

Introduce the idea of an imaginary game of basketball – show them an imaginary ball and your dribbling technique!

Say: 'I will start by passing the imaginary ball to someone across the room. [Identify this person by name or by pointing towards them.] As soon as I pass the ball the rumble starts, and as soon as the ball is received by my team mate, the rumble stops.' You need to explain that the distances between people are like on a basketball court, so don't receive the ball too quickly – it can take a while to reach people – and participants should catch the ball clearly. Follow the ball with your eyes and between passes do pretend bounces.

Note: Stay alert to people being left out of this game.

Advanced
Age Range: 10 years and up.

Divide the group into two teams – have every second group member move their chair back slightly to differentiate who is in which team (the circle stays intact). Then have each team choose their 'defence guard' – they must be seated roughly opposite each other.

The game proceeds with people passing the ball to each other using the same naming technique and rumble as in the initial version (identify the person by name or by pointing towards them). Anytime after three passes, a person can shoot at the goal – to shoot at the goal you don't have to say a name but you do have to voice the word 'Shoot' and look towards the goalie – practise some passing and shooting. To protect their goal, the 'defence guard' has to play a specific rhythm immediately after the word 'Shoot' comes from the attacker's lips – I try to make the complexity of this rhythm match the capacity of the group, but often use a five Bass rumble followed by three quick Flams (BbBbB – fl,fl,fl). This will deflect the ball and it is then taken by the defending team. If the goalie makes a mistake with the rhythm or is slow to respond, it becomes a goal and again the ball changes sides. Remember each time there must be a minimum of three passes before someone can shoot at the goal.

1 + 2 + 3 + 4 +	1 + 2 + 3 + 4 +
B b B b B	fl fl fl -

(C) RUMBLE SOLO

The group plays a steady 4/4 foundation rhythm and the facilitator counts down to stop the rhythm ('4, 3, 2, 1, STOP'). In the break between stopping and restarting the rhythm, one person rumbles for three counts before the group begins again on the first note of the new bar. At first do the break and mark the three rests with three claps – this will help with timing – before replacing the claps with rumbles.

First practise stopping for the three counts and resuming on the first note of the next bar. Once this is achieved consistently, group members take it in turns to rumble across this break.

Adaptions: Solo of choice in the break. Extend the break to seven counts.

12.1.3 Introductory Games

IND, GRP, FAM, COR. Age Range: 8 years and up.

Key Focus Areas: Group familiarity, vocalisation, rhythmic timing and coordination.

(A) RHYTHM NAME PASS

Start a simple rhythm in sets of three O o O - B b B - O o O - B b B (add percussion instruments as well if you have them). Choose one person to start and have them say their own name and follow that with another person's name (from the group) without losing the rhythm. The person they chose then takes up the mantle, repeating their own name and saying another person's name, and so the naming moves around the circle – every time someone loses the rhythm while speaking everyone changes place in the circle and gets to try a new instrument.

1 + 2 + 3 + 4 +	1 + 2 + 3 + 4 +
O o O B b B	O o O B b B

(B) THE INTRODUCTORY NAME GAME

Ask each person to turn to the person next to them and ask them one thing that makes them feel safe.

Then start a soft Bass pulse and have each person introduce their new associate using the phrases:

'I talked to…[insert name]' and 'Everyone meet…[insert name]'.

Then finish with the phrase: '[Insert name]… feels safe when…'

Write the names and their safety examples on the white-board and discuss the importance of safety in different areas of life.

(C) WHAT DO YOU KNOW ABOUT?

Ask each person to turn to the person next to them, introduce themselves and tell them one of their passions. If the group is already known to each other, replace this question with one thing that they feel strongly about and one thing you didn't previously know about them.

Then start a simple, soft, foundation rhythm and tell the group you will ask them a question with the drum phrase: fl - O o O o O - fl (What do you know, about…), and one at a time they should answer your question with two Bass notes that complete the phrase (e.g. fl - O o O o O - fl - B B) and then tell the group what they found out from the person they spoke with.

1 + 2 + 3 + 4 +	1 + 2 + 3 + 4 +
fl OoOoO	fl
1 + 2 + 3 + 4 +	1 + 2 + 3 + 4 +
fl OoOoO	fl B B -

Practise the rhythm and the answering Bass notes a few times before beginning the exercise. You should ask each person in turn, one at a time, using the rhythm above. Each time you add the question, the rhythm should stop. The chosen individual should then answer with the two Bass notes and tell you and the rest of the group what they learned. Then the foundation rhythm resumes.

Note: I often find everyone gets into the habit of joining me in the questioning drum phrase.

You can also change the nature of these questions and use this exercise to increase group participation at any point of the program (Think, Pair, Share).

(D) MORE THAN A NAME
ADAPTED FROM M. COLLARD

Age Range: Older youth and adults – 12 years and up.

Have each person introduce themselves to the group by reversing their name and making up an explanation of what their new name means – for example, Simon says: 'Hello, my name is "Nomis" and my name means "I never miss".' The group drums the person's name back to them – accenting the syllables to the beat, for example O - O -, and repeating it so it forms an ongoing rhythm.

NO MIS	I Never Miss
O - O -	O o O o

(E) SAY YOUR NAME AND PLAY YOUR NAME
This is a generic rhythm naming game where one at a time each person plays their name, aligning beats to the syllables, until it becomes a repetitive rhythm. The whole group joins in the rhythm of that name for a set number of measures and then a new name is converted in the same way.

Note: This exercise draws on a useful music-teaching skill that uses words to reinforce rhythms. If at any stage an individual is struggling to learn a particular rhythm, adding a reinforcing vocal accompaniment may help.

12.1.4 Rhythm Coordination Games

IND, GRP, FAM, COR. Age Range: 8 years and up.

Key Focus Areas: Drumming technique, coordination, balance, focus and attention, body awareness, group familiarity, teamwork, visualisation.

(A) BASS, TONE AND FLAM

Issues Addressed: Hand-drum technique, motor coordination.

Introduce the technique of playing the Bass, Tone and Flam (see Sections 10.4 and 10.5) and then tell everybody that in this next game the key rule is that they can only be played in this order (Bass, Tone, Flam).

You are going to pass one strike of the drum, in that order, around the room – get participants to practise the technique of hitting the drum with one hand and pointing to another individual at the same time (a motor coordination exercise).

Choose one person to start. They should begin with a single Bass note – at the same time, they should point to another person who must play a Tone while pointing to another who must play a Flam. The game continues until someone plays the wrong note out of turn. Each time someone does this, the group rumbles and that person starts off a new round with a Bass note.

Try passing between one Bass, followed by two Tones and three Flams, with the aim being to get this patterns happening smoothly like a rhythm.

B, OO, flflfl – B, OO, flflfl

Variations: Replace the Flam with a Slap or add both to make it a four sound combination.

(B) STRETCH TO THE RHYTHM

Play a steady foundation rhythm with one hand and move through a series of stretches and other movements with the other. Variations may include:

- Roll your neck, so it's nice and loose.

- Lift and lower your chin, then turn your head from side to side.

- Roll your shoulders.

- Arch your back, then slouch forward – rock between the two.

- Move your chest from side to side, keeping your head still.

- Lift the knees one at a time.

- Extend the legs one at a time.

- Extend the non-playing arm.

- Make a circular wrist motion of the non-playing hand, clockwise and anti-clockwise.

Finish with a rumble.

Ask your participant/s if there are any moves they want to try.

(C) BALANCE ME

Have a select number of your group enter the middle of the circle.

On a specific signal from the drum, they must change their stance as follows:

- One Bass note – stand on one leg.

- Two Bass notes – swap from one leg to the other.

- One Tone note – stand on one leg with the other at 90 degrees.

- Two Tone notes – stand on one leg and hold the knee.

- Any three notes – rest.

One at a time, each remaining member of the group should play one of the signals on their drum and the people in the middle should respond.

Adapt these movements to the capacity of your group members, and where relevant, encourage them to lean on each other for support. Where else might you need the support of others to find balance in your life?

Discuss the importance of balance to health, including both physical and psychological health.

(D) TAG (YOU'RE IT!) WITH RHYTHM

GRP only. Age Range: 8–18 years.

One person is chosen as 'It' (the person who tags others). In this game the tag is placed on another person by pointing at that person with one hand (and if possible saying their name) while maintaining the group rhythm with the other hand (it can be good to add the extra challenge that the pointing hand must cross the drumming hand – see the image below).

$$1 + 2 + 3 + 4 + \qquad 1 + 2 + 3 + 4 +$$

$$\text{B} \quad \text{O} \quad \text{B} \quad \text{O} \qquad \text{B} \quad \text{O} \quad \text{B} \quad \text{O}$$

A simple, one-handed foundation pattern such as BOBO is sufficient for the underlying group rhythm. The one who is being tagged can resist the tag by playing three Bass notes without losing their rhythm – practise this before starting the game.

If someone loses their rhythm whilst tagging someone, then the tag doesn't stick. If someone loses their rhythm while trying to play the three Bass notes (i.e. trying to resist the tag), then the tag will stick.

(E) SEE IT, THEN PLAY IT

In drumming, a common way to learn a new rhythm is to say it and then play it – the vocal phrasing reinforces the motor skills required to play the pattern.

In other contexts, we can often improve our performance and stimulate our creativity by imagining or visualising a scenario or event occurring.

Try saying a rhythm and then playing it.

Ask participants to visualise a rhythm (emphasise closing their eyes, picturing the rhythm in as much detail as possible and feeling themselves playing it on their imaginary drum). Give them two minutes to picture themselves playing a new beat (it can be useful to close the eyes).

Ask for volunteers to play their rhythm and have everyone join them.

Discuss the use of visualisation in helping people focus and problem solve. Visualisation is a mental practice, and research has found that in many cases it is as effective as the real thing.

(F) WHAT SOUND WAS THAT?

Specialist Population: Sensory perception disorders, sound localisation problems.

Hand out a range of percussion instruments – one for each person. Ask one person to shut their eyes, then point to one person and have them play their instrument for a brief period. The person with their eyes closed must guess what type of instrument was being played.

Adaption

Extend this game by having the person with their eyes shut situated in the middle of the circle and the facilitator asking one person in the outer circle to play their instrument – the person in the middle must track down the sound, moving towards it and stopping opposite the person playing it.

Extend this version by doing the same exercise, but this time everyone should play at once and the person in the middle must track down the one sound amongst all the others.

12.1.5 Boundaries

IND, GRP, FAM, COR. Age Range: 5 years and up.

Key Focus Areas: Values, boundary awareness, protective behaviours, social confidence, communication, healthy relationships.

This exercise can be used to help establish boundaries for an ongoing program as well as to explore boundaries generally and protective behaviours specifically.

(A) HANDS OFF!
USE THIS TO ESTABLISH GROUP GUIDELINES
Part 1

Open up a discussion on boundaries in relationships; what role they perform, why they are needed, how difficult it can be to enforce them, etc. Say: 'Often drummers are wary of other people playing their favourite drum and put boundaries around who can use it.'

What might make a drummer choose whether to allow someone to play their favourite drum?

In the first part of this exercise one person should put their hands on the drum of the person next to them (in groups this will be every second person in the circle).

The aim is to look at different non-verbal ways in which we can protect or reinforce our boundaries and let the person know we don't want their hand there.

Demonstrate a range of non-verbal options – for example, frowning, huffing, shaking your head, glaring, moving your drum or moving their hand.

Inform those with their hand on the drum that they are to remove it when their partner registers their disapproval by using one of these signals – let the exercise begin.

Why are boundaries important? What sorts of boundaries might you want to maintain in a healthy relationship? How do your values influence your boundaries? If you weren't sure of your values, would that mean your boundaries might be uncertain?

Part 2

The second part looks at verbal signals to protect or reinforce boundaries. Demonstrate some verbal signals – for example: 'Get your hand off my drum', 'Please remove your hand', 'I'm not comfortable with you touching my drum', etc. Swap roles so that the opposite person now has their hand on their partner's drum and practise using verbal techniques (the person should remove their hand on being told to do so).

How do you know what's right or wrong? How do you tell someone when they have crossed your boundary? Do you know people who don't really understand boundaries?

Part 3

This time, swap again, but the person with their hand on the other person's drum should not be easily dissuaded. Participants are going to have to be really clear and firm to get the person to remove their hand – they should use both non-verbal and verbal techniques.

How did it feel to have someone resist your boundary? What helped convince them to remove their hand? What did it feel like to cross another person's boundary? What are the boundaries we need to reinforce in this relationship of ours or in this group? Write these on a white-board and review the group's adherence to them across future sessions.

Explore the four-step process for communicating when someone encroaches upon your personal boundaries.

1. Name the behaviour.

2. Give a clear direction.

3. Repeat that direction.

4. Escape if necessary.

12.2 Social and Emotional Learning

Social and emotional learning (SEL) is now recognised as a key focus within the national school curriculum, with research demonstrating that increased levels of social and emotional awareness and understanding improve school climate, academic performance and student behaviour. SEL competencies include recognising and managing our emotions, developing healthy relationships with others, making healthy and well-informed choices and taking responsibility for our actions.

12.2.1 Values

IND, GRP, FAM, COR. Age Range: 8 years and up.

Key Focus Areas: Identifying values, peer pressure, teamwork, healthy relationships.

(A) FINDING FIVE (OR MORE)

Ask people to list the key things of value or fundamental importance to them on a white-board (give examples if people get stuck). Identify those values that are common between people and settle on a core of five.

Then teach the break Finding Five (O o O o O - B b B b B), which represents attending to those five core values.

Call	Answer
1 + 2 + 3 + 4 +	1 + 2 + 3 + 4 +
O o O o O	B b B b B

Divide the group in two so that half play the Tones and half play the Bass, or in individual work the practitioner plays one and the individual they are working with the other.

A rhythm is played and a break of five Tone notes is inserted, answered by five Bass notes – repeat another three times (four in total) before returning to your rhythm.

How important is it to be able to identify our values clearly? Why? What helped you work out your values? How do values govern the way we act? How easy is it for you to stick to your values?

Variation: You can change the break so that the last time you repeat the sequence (the 4th time) the first half of the group begin with their Tones and the whole group answer with three Bass notes followed by the group yelling out the name of one key value before returning to the foundation rhythm.

(B) THE VALUES RHYTHM

Draw up a list of values on the white-board, and ask each person to choose one that is important to them. Then demonstrate how to use the syllables of each to make it into a rhythm, for example: Truth – one beat, Love – one beat, Kindness – two beats, Respect – two beats, Forgiveness – three beats, Honesty – three beats, Generosity – five beats.

Each person has to play a rhythm representing a value that is important to them and connect it to the others in the group.

Start the exercise by playing your 'value rhythm' and then have each person enter with their 'value rhythm' one at a time. (They can be encouraged to say or sing the name of their value to their beat as they enter.)

How do values connect people? What if your values were very different from someone else's? Would it be easy or difficult to get on with someone whose values were different from yours?

(C) HOLD ONTO YOUR VALUES

Sometimes we lose hold of our values, especially when we are with people who don't have the same values as ourselves or when we are under pressure. Remember your value rhythm from before.

One at a time, each person should play their 'value rhythm' (ask them to play it using two hands if possible) at a set tempo, and the rest of the group should try to distract that player with different beats and tempos.

Initially try distracting the player with random beats and then try it as a unified group – playing a contrasting rhythm together.

If it is hard to resist group pressure and a person loses their way (i.e. gets drawn away from their value rhythm), then you can stop the group and try the same exercise again, but with the person under threat getting more support (i.e. other people joining them in their values rhythm).

What are some of the situations where you might find your values under threat? What might help you hold onto them when you come under pressure to abandon them? Does having other people stand up for the same values help strengthen yours? Are there times when you might need to compromise your values?

(D) CROSSING THE LINE 12.4.2

Use this exercise to examine values, boundaries and behaviour.

12.2.2 Awareness

IND, GRP, FAM. Age Range: 8 years and up.

Key Focus Areas: Emotional awareness, focus and attention.

(A) SHOW SOME EMOTION

The group (or client and counsellor) should play a rhythm of their choice through a range of emotional states (about 15 seconds for each feeling). One at a time, each person should contribute a new feeling and name that feeling before the group shifts to join them; and so it continues, moving on to the next person in the group after 15 seconds or so. Facilitators may also ask how each feeling impacted the group or individual before moving on to the next one.

Can playing these feelings provide any insight into how they impact us?

(B) MINDFUL AWARENESS SCRIPT – SOUND

Use a simple and very soft Bass pulse (40–60 bpm) or the Rhythmic Wave exercise (Chapter 11) as the focal point for this awareness exercise. Give instructions in a mellow, clear voice, speaking slowly and in time to the rhythm. Remember, the script below is just a guide – make it your own.

- Relax your body.

- Adjust your body until you feel comfortable and relaxed. You may wish to close your eyes or focus on one spot. Focus on and relax any tension in your neck, shoulders, chest, arms, hands, back, hips, thighs, lower legs, feet.

- Slow your breathing – focus on your breath, in and out, aligning it to the pulse, becoming still.

- Now focus solely on sounds. Listen to the Bass note of the rhythm first.

- Listen to it in all its dimensions – tone, pitch, frequency. Listen to it in its primacy as pure sound, rather than naming it.

- If other thoughts come to mind, acknowledge them briefly and move your focus back to the sound of the Bass note.

- If you feel comfortable, let the vibrations of the Bass note move through your body, grounding you.

- Breathe gently, slowly.

- Let those vibrations travel down to your feet and exit into the floor, connecting you to the earth.

- Now focus on any other sounds. Experience loud and soft sounds, obvious and not so obvious sounds and the gap between sounds.

- Try to avoid categorising these sounds but experience them as raw energy. If other thoughts come to mind, acknowledge them briefly and move your focus back to the sounds of your environment.

- Breathe gently, slowly.

- Slowly come back to a focus on the Bass.

- Hold your focus on the Bass and allow the volume to slowly fade away.

If possible, sit in silence for 40–60 seconds; or if part of the Rhythmic Wave exercise, you can move back into the improvised rhythm play you started from.

12.2.3 Thoughts and Feelings

IND, GRP, FAM, COR. Age Range: 8 years and up.

Key Focus Areas: Emotional Awareness, positivity, hope, peer pressure, unhealthy relationships, empowerment, self-responsibility.

(A) ACCENT THE POSITIVE

Ask the individual or participants you are working with to come up with one good thing in their lives – give examples (it may be their friends, or it could be something as fundamental as still being alive). Ask them to come up with one positive thing that has happened to them this week, then narrow it down to today (e.g. 'It wasn't raining' or 'I got here safely').

Introduce 'Call and Response' and showcase one specific pattern that will serve as representing the positive things that happen to people in their lives. If you play that rhythm, people must play a loud accent note – fl,fl – on their instrument to mark it. Other rhythms are to be responded to normally as a direct echo.

$$1 + 2 + 3 + 4 +$$

$$- \quad fl \quad fl \quad -$$

Start the game and throw in the chosen part sporadically and in ways that may be hard to hear (low volume, different hand technique).

Discuss the challenges of staying positive and the 'Losada principle 3:1', which states that we need to hear three positives to balance one negative in order to maintain a healthy self-concept. Why are we often over-conscious of the negatives in life? How can we train ourselves to focus more on what is going right in our lives, or what we do that's right?

Note: Some groups choose to start each session with this exercise as a way of reinforcing the practice of staying positive.

(B) KEEP YOUR DISTANCE!

GRP, FAM, COR. Issue Addressed: Bullying

Start by briefly discussing the impact of other people's negativity on your mood and behaviour, and the challenges of distancing yourself from negative influences.

Agree on a simple pattern to represent a negative influence. One person should be blindfolded in the middle of the circle and told that they need to keep away from the negative rhythm (choose one particular rhythm to represent a negative influence, e.g. five tones OoOoO). Then the group should play a simple rhythm, with one person chosen to play the negative rhythm – the person in the middle needs to back away from this player. The rhythm can then be passed to a new drummer, usually by eye contact, so that more and more players are exerting the negative energy and it becomes harder and harder for the person in the middle to escape its influence.

Then stop and discuss how that felt for the person in the middle: 'Has anyone had that feeling of not being able to get away before?' Now showcase a 'Rhythm of Courage' – a different short and sharp pattern that will complement the existing two parts, for example:

$$1 + 2 + 3 + 4 + \qquad\qquad 1 + 2 + 3 + 4 +$$

$$O \; o \; O \; o \; O \qquad\qquad O \; o \; O \; o \; O$$

The group are told that they are going to repeat the exercise with a new volunteer in the middle, but this time anyone not co-opted by the bullies can play a rescue rhythm – a rhythm of courage – representing standing up against bullying and a place of safety.

This rhythm of courage becomes a place, or places, of safety within the circle, and the person in the middle can escape the bullying by gravitating towards this rhythm when played.

When people bring you down, what can you do about it? How hard is it to distance yourself from the negative impact of others? Have you found that negativity, cynicism or anger are emotions that multiply, infecting others? Do you ever feel as if there is no escape? How can we stay alert and protect ourselves from these influences? What about courage – how hard is it to stand up for what is right? What can you do to help this?

Relate this game to identifying dangers in different contexts such as:

- bullying – getting drawn into treating others badly

- drug use – negative peer group, peer pressure, environmental triggers, stress

- relationships – selfishness, inattention, non-communication, violence.

12.2.4 Smart Choices

IND, GRP, FAM, COR. Age Range: 8 years and up.

Key Focus Areas: Empowerment, motivation, peer pressure.

(A) IT'S YOUR CHOICE

The practitioner should start a rhythm and each person should be given the option of joining the rhythm by playing the same as the practitioner or finding their own rhythm that connects to the underlying pulse (representing core values). The practitioner should increase the complexity of the rhythm (representing a complex issue), notifying all participants that they can choose to follow or connect using a different part of their own.

Discuss the subject of 'choice' – what made you decide which path to follow? How easy is it to get pulled into unmanageable situations like a complex rhythm? Did you get caught up in the rhythm? How often do we make poor choices because we get caught up in something without thinking it through? How hard is it to distance yourself at times like this, so that you can make good choices? How hard was it to find an alternative choice (rhythm)? What helped you maintain the connection?

(B) HOLD ONTO YOUR RHYTHM

Note: Don't initially warn the client that they are to try to hold steady.

Ask an individual to play a rhythm of their choice on their drum that they think they can hold steady (encourage using two hands where possible). Ask them to maintain that rhythm while you start an alternative rhythm (have everyone play this if in a group).

See whether the person comes over to your pattern or not. If they lose their rhythm, start again and ask them to focus on holding out against the influence of the alternative rhythm.

Discuss peer pressure scenarios – what influences a person to do things or not at the instigation of their peers? How important was focus, willpower, etc. to avoid getting drawn into the alternative rhythm? Can friends help in situations like this?

12.2.5 Emotional Control

IND, GRP, FAM, COR. Age Range: 8 years and up.

Key Focus Areas: Emotional Awareness, problem solving, emotional regulation, personal agency.

(A) THE PRESSURE POT

First, discuss with the group the things they feel put them under pressure, worry them or cause them anxiety. Ask them to think of one thing each, and as they enter the rhythm call it out loud. Provide some relevant examples, depending on the nature of who you are working with.

One at a time, starting with the facilitator, the group members should enter the rhythm – start slow. Each time, a person yells out their stressor before joining the rhythm; and each time a new person joins, the tempo should increase. Keep the rhythm volume low so that the people's words can be heard.

By the time the final person enters, the tempo should be almost unmanageable (overwhelming – as in how we feel when we are emotionally overloaded).

Finish with a rumble. If there are noticeable signs of distress, extend the exercise with a calming breathing activity.

Did you notice any similarities in the types of things that make people feel stressed? How did it feel to be part of the rhythm as the tempo quickened? Did you feel you may have been losing control? In times like these what do you do to regain control?

Note: This exercise is generally run in conjunction with the 'Pressure Valve' exercise below.

(B) THE PRESSURE VALVE

First, discuss with your group all the things that help reduce their stress when they feel down or worried. Ask them to think of one thing each and as they enter the rhythm to yell that out.

One at a time, starting with the facilitator, the group members should enter the rhythm – start at a fast tempo. Each new person should enter by first yelling out their 'relaxer' and then joining in with their drum. Each time a new person enters, the tempo should slow slightly.

By the time the last person enters, the rhythm should be very slow. Finish by slowly fading the rhythm away.

There has always been stress in life, but now it is at unprecedented levels. What choices can you make to reduce the stress level in your life? Does avoiding stressful situations have the potential to make them more stressful than they need to be? How might acceptance help you manage stress?

(C) CONTRASTING EMOTIONS

List a range of emotions on a white-board – you can have people contribute to this list.

Divide your group in two; or in individual therapy, divide roles between the counsellor and the individual. Ask people to define contrasting emotions as in the following table.

Unpleasant emotions	Pleasant emotions
Sad	Content
Disgust	Inspired
Angry	Joyful
Contempt	Love

Choose an accessible rhythm (one you can play comfortably) and then have each side choose a different contrasting emotion and transfer that into their playing – thus the same rhythm is played with two different feelings. Swap roles so that in each instance different sides are playing the uplifting emotion.

Discuss the feelings these different emotions evoke, the contrasts between them and how they interact together in rhythm and in life. What was the impact of one emotion on the other? Were particular emotions dominant? Can we use contrasting emotions to limit the impact of more problematic feelings? Did you gain any insights into the nature of different feelings by playing with them in this way?

(D) THE ECHO WAVE
A USEFUL REGULATION EXERCISE

Set a direction around the circle or move back and forth between yourself as the counsellor and the individual you are working with. One at a time, each person should repeat the pattern you play, getting slightly softer each time. The aim is to reduce the volume evenly until the last person in the circle plays a barely heard beat. Each time you try to perfect it, start with a new person and a new pattern.

Then see if you can start a wave pattern, with the group starting soft, building up by the middle person (or in individual work, by the middle of the exercise) and then de-escalating.

Finally, try this wave pattern so that it continues endlessly – beginning soft, rising in the middle, tailing off and then beginning the same pattern over again as a flow.

Note: Also try this with the tonal chimes (use a pentatonic scale, CDEGA).

Utilise this exercise to explore the cyclical nature of life in different areas (e.g. moods, relationships, success/failure, youth, old age, etc.). Have you noticed that many elements of life have a cyclical nature? Have you seen this in some of your own relationships? Does this provide you with any hope for those times when life is difficult? Is it realistic to expect that things will always be up? How does this relate to the concept of balance in life?

(E) DROP IT

Teach everyone to play the different parts of a rhythm from the rhythm catalogue (Chapter 10) and explain that you will ask each person to remove one note from their rhythm by holding one finger high in the air. Give some examples of how a rhythm might sound as you pare back the notes.

Start the rhythm and have each subgroup remove one note each at a time; hold this new incarnation for a while and then ask them to remove a further note. Follow this routine until you have a sparse, ambient rhythm. Fade slowly away.

Sometimes when we let things go, we bring more clarity and peace into our lives. How easy is it to let go of things in your life that are stressing you or are not really necessary? What about the influence of others that might be hurting you in some way – can you let them go? What about your thoughts and feelings that bring you down – how might you reduce their influence? Discuss the use of mindful acceptance here.

Variation: Try this with tonal chimes.

12.2.6 Tolerance and Understanding

IND, GRP, FAM, COR. Age Range: 5 years and up.

Key Focus Areas: Universality, tolerance, healthy relationships, communication.

(A) UP AND DOWN

Ask one person to play a slow, steady pulse on the Bass note of their drum (they are the co-facilitator).

Say: 'In this game I am going to go through a list of statements and you are going to stand up if they are true about you and stay seated if not – try to stand and sit on the pulse of the Bass note, not in between the notes.'

Make a series of statements relevant to your group that promote tolerance:

- Stand if you have a friend who is different from you.

- Stand if you speak two languages.

- Stand if you like football.

- Stand if you ever get lonely.

- Stand if you live with one parent.

- Stand if you like ice cream.

- Stand if you like to win.

- Stand if you like to get your own way.

- Stand if you like music.

- Stand if you ever get angry.

Adapt the questions to the participants' age range and interests. Replace standing and sitting with other indicators, such as different drum responses, for those with physical difficulties that make standing difficult.

Have a discussion on the things that make us human, things that unite us and things that divide us. Did you notice how many of these questions we answered together? As people do you think we are more alike or less alike? Why do you think we sometimes focus more on the differences between us than on recognising our similarities?

Note: Amend the questions to suit the issues of the individual or group.

(B) PUT UPS – WHAT I LIKE ABOUT YOU

GRP, FAM, COR.

Discuss the propensity to find fault with other people, particularly those who might be different from us. Like getting caught in an unhealthy pattern (rhythm), we need to watch how we judge others and try to focus on the positives if we are to develop healthy relationships. Think about the person next to you and find one thing about them you value.

Start with a simple foundation rhythm from Section 10.8, and then, addressing one person at a time, add the break O o O o O - fl (What I like about you), which stops the rhythm and is followed by the same person stating what that quality is (e.g. Tom is always kind to other people). Then everyone should return to the simple foundation rhythm.

$$1 + 2 + 3 + 4 +$$
$$O o O o O \quad fl$$

How hard is it say nice things about someone to their face? How often do you remember to do that? What does it feel like to say positive things to your friends and family? What about when people pay you compliments? Are there risks in being more positive towards other people? What else makes it hard to be more positive? What might help?

12.2.7 Positive Relationships

IND, GRP, FAM, COR. Age Range: 8 years and up.

Key Focus Areas: Healthy relationships, values, communication.

(A) BALANCE BEAT
The counsellor should work with the client (or divide a larger group into pairs), with the focus being to create a two-part harmony that includes some of the elements of a balanced, healthy relationship.

Discuss what those elements might be before breaking off into pairs to develop a rhythm.

Give participants around four to five minutes to come back with a rhythm, which they play, one pair at a time, to the group. The rhythm should contain at least one original pattern.

Together, analyse each two-part rhythm for the different qualities of a healthy relationships – respect, balance, listening, connection, fun, etc.

The group as a whole can be divided down the middle to play any of these new rhythms, with each half of the group playing one part.

(B) A RHYTHMIC CONVERSATION

Discuss the following: What are the elements of good communication? Why is good communication so fundamental to healthy relationships?

One person should be asked to choose someone in the group and start a conversation with that person using their drum, to which the other person should respond. Analyse the conversation for the following elements – balance, listening, dominance and respect.

What are some of the elements of poor communication we can all fall into? How can this impact our relationships? Why? How can we improve our communication skills?

12.2.8 Care and Empathy

IND, GRP, FAM, COR. Age Range: 8 years and up.

Key Focus Areas: Universality, empathy, emotional awareness, healthy relationships, social awareness.

Issues Addressed: Social referencing. Specialist Populations: Autism, Asperger's syndrome.

(A) IMAGINE IT WAS YOU
The facilitator should describe a number of experiences (positive and challenging) and ask the group to rumble on their drum if they can identify with each of the emotions that might be garnered for an individual experiencing that event.
Examples:

- Imagine you just kicked the winning goal in the grand final – rumble if you might feel excited, proud, etc.

- Imagine if people always put you down – rumble if you might feel sad, angry, etc.

- Imagine you won the lottery – rumble if you might feel excited, happy, relieved, etc.

- Imagine if your best friend just left town – rumble if you might feel let down, sad, dejected, betrayed, etc.

Discuss the concept of empathy. What is empathy? How does it affect the way we act towards others? What if people have little empathy?

THE EMOTIONAL DETECTIVE
A USEFUL EXERCISE FOR EMOTIONAL RECOGNITION

Give each person in the group an emotion (from a list you have previously identified with the group). One person should be chosen as the detective and stand in the middle of the circle and choose someone to expresses their chosen feeling using their drum, facial features or both. If the detective identifies the feeling correctly, they swap places with the individual who shared their emotion – if not, the group helps out and the detective gets another go to test their emotional detection skills.

In one-to-one work the practitioner and the person they work with should swap roles between being the detective and the person who will express the feeling.

Adaption: The detective can be blindfolded and asked to describe the emotion unsighted the first time, and if incorrect given another opportunity with the blindfold removed – this adaption provides scope to explore the role of body language in identifying feelings.

Discuss the challenge of interpreting others' emotions and the implications of misreading another's feelings. What helped you interpret these feelings? How easy is it to mask what you are feeling from others? If it is fairly easy, does that make it hard for people to understand each other sometimes? How important is it to be honest about our feelings with those closest to us?

(C) HELP ME OUT, IF YOU CAN (FL FL FL O O O)

$$1 + 2 + 3 + \qquad 1 + 2 + 3 +$$

$$\text{fl} \quad \text{fl} \quad \text{fl} \qquad \text{O} \quad \text{o} \quad \text{O}$$

Note: This is not suitable for individual sessions.

Start with a short discussion on the importance of helping out others if you can and getting help yourself when you need it – everyone has the potential to do both and each brings rewards. It can be difficult to give and it can also be difficult to ask for help. What are some of the situations where you might need support or be able to offer support?

One person should start a simple foundation rhythm and each person should enter in succession but only at the request of the drummer already playing next to them. The drummer should invite the next person to join the group with the phrase 'Help me out, if you can!', (fl, fl, fl, – O o O). When everyone is in, finish with all players doing the break and saying the phrase 'Help me out if you can!' at the same time.

1 + 2 + 3 +   1 + 2 + 3 +

fl fl fl   O o O

Discuss the benefits of altruism. What are the rewards of giving or supporting someone in times of need? If giving brings rewards, why is it often hard to ask for help? How does balance impact this issue? Can you ask too much or give too much?

12.2.9 Giving Back

IND, GRP, FAM, COR. Age Range: 8 years and up.

Key Focus Areas: Creativity, healthy relationships, teamwork, altruism, self-care.

(A) GIVE AND TAKE

Use improvisation, with each person adding their own rhythm to the group.

Layer in the rhythm, one person at a time. After playing for a few minutes, stop and look at how the different contributions and support of each person help to strengthen the community (group rhythm). Repeat the process, but this time, when the rhythm is in full motion, ask each person to stop playing one by one until the song is ended. Then examine the consequences of people withdrawing from community, reducing their support, etc.

Discuss different ways people give and take in their relationships and where the balance may lie. Can families, communities or teams really thrive without everybody chipping in and pulling their weight? When people do contribute and support each other in pursuit of a common goal, how much quicker is that goal realised? Why is that? What happens when people don't pull their weight or just 'take' all the time?

(B) BUDDIES

Pair people up directly across the circle and give them the challenge of coming up with a pattern they could not play on their own. In individual therapy, the practitioner and the individual should work on this together. Allow about five minutes.

Then, if you are in a group, have each pair play their pattern to the remaining participants and follow that by teaching the rhythm so that the whole group can join in, with half of the group playing one part and the other half playing its counter-part (this usually means individuals from each pair will teach, play and lead half the group each in a different part of the rhythm they made up).

What allows people to work together like this? What are some of the skills involved? How challenging was it? What made it work? What other aspects of your life require these same skills?

(C) RUMBLE FOR THE GIVING

Ask your participants to think about one thing they enjoy doing that gives back or helps out another person or community. Give some examples: maybe you enjoy lending your friends some lunch money; maybe you enjoy helping out around the house; maybe you enjoy standing up for your friends when they are being bullied.

Then have each person ask one question of the rest of the group about whether they too enjoy the same type of giving – for example, 'Rumble if you enjoy…'

What are the rewards of giving back? Why do we sometimes hold back offering others our help if we know that giving brings these rewards? Can you be taken advantage of sometimes if you are a generous person? What would happen if we all stopped giving and focused only on taking?

(D) GIVING AND RECEIVING

Divide the group in two, or in individual work move between the counsellor and the individual they are working with. Using tonal chimes (pentatonic scale), have half the group play as a gift to the other half.

Ask the giving group to extend their music as a gift to the other half – to play for them with consideration and generosity.

Play for around three to five minutes and ask the receiving group to relax and focus on receiving and appreciating this gift from the other. Swap roles.

Discuss how it felt to give and to receive. Discuss the rewards and challenges of giving and receiving. How do our judgments limit us when giving or receiving? How does balance impact this?

12.2.10 Managing Adversity

IND, GRP, FAM, COR. Age Range: 8 years and up.

Key Focus Areas: Social justice, resilience, empathy, hope, listening skills, teamwork, social support, creativity, problem solving.

May not be suitable for the elderly or disabled.

(A) BOUNCE BACK (BACK ON TRACK)

Find an example of someone who has been treated unfairly and risen above it to achieve great things. Examples close to home work best, but celebrities or sports stars can also be useful.

Say: 'In this exercise we are going to hear one rhythm that knocks us down (unfairness) and play one rhythm that sets us back on our feet (resilience). As you slump low, think about the types of things that "get you down"; and as you rise up out of your chair, 'think about what helps you "bounce back"'.

'We start with a simple, steady rhythm from the rhythm catalogue and when you hear the facilitator's call [12 quick Tones followed by a sharp Flam] you have to stop playing and slump in your chairs as low as possible – after an 8-count pause [practitioner counts these out aloud], you stand up straight playing three strong Bass notes (Back on Track) and then resume your seat and re-enter the rhythm.'

Demonstrate the timing of the break – 12 counts from stop to go (8 counts of slumping and 4 counts standing up and then re-joining the rhythm).

What are some of the things that can knock people down and take away their confidence and hope? What are some of the ways people pick themselves back up? Can you give an example of 'bounce back'? If possible, have each person list a situation of their own where they have bounced back from adversity.

Note: This can be adapted for people with a physical disability.

(B) ONE DOOR CLOSES AND ANOTHER OPENS

Explain to the group or the individual you are working with that you will all start with a three-time rhythm from the rhythm catalogue (Chapter 10), and at any time the practitioner can indicate to a player that the door is shut (looking at them and saying or mouthing 'door shut'). When that happens, the player must stop and reassess the situation and enter with a new rhythm that complements the existing pattern (the whole group may then join the new rhythm or can continue with the existing pattern). Now that they have re-entered the rhythm (door open), that player gets to choose the next person on whom the door will shut, and so the game proceeds.

Note: Be sensitive to closing the door on people – ensure people understand this is an exercise and are comfortable being shut out. Also emphasise that this rhythm may be tricky to enter and they may need to try different patterns until finding one that works – a fall back position is to connect via the Bass note (representing healthy values).

Have a discussion on the fact that doors never really close but may appear to – if we look closely, there is a lesson or an opportunity available each time. Can you think of an example where one door shut on you but another opened?

What can you do if doors keep shutting on you all the time? How easy is it to adapt your rhythm to new opportunities? What are the dangers of sticking to the same old routines?

(C) FIND YOUR WAY HOME – LISTEN FOR THE SILENCE
ADAPTED FROM ARTHUR HULL

Specialist Population: Sensory perception disorders.

Everyone should play the heartbeat rhythm of their choice (see Section 10.9) while one member at a time enters the circle blindfolded and tries to locate their empty chair – prior to searching, they turn on the spot three times to disorientate themselves. Focus on soft drumming.

Lead a discussion on finding a reference point to get back home or to a place of safety when you feel lost, down and out, or disorientated. What helped you locate your empty chair? How important was it not to give up? How important was it to trust yourself? Did you get support from others in any way? Did you have to rely on your own ingenuity? What did it feel like if you couldn't get back?

Note: May not be suitable for aged care groups or people with a physical disability.

12.3 Identity and Culture

This section looks at issues of belonging – where we fit within our communities, our sense of who we are and our obligations and responsibilities as family and community members. Many people have lost their sense of identity and community membership, whether through cultural displacement or the ever-changing nature of modern life. Having a strong sense of one's identity, including one's ethnic culture, acts as a protective factor, even buffering the effects of poverty and discrimination (Garcia Coll and Marks, 2009). This section aims to help individuals increase their sense of self and place and, through this, improve self-confidence, self-respect and cultural understanding.

12.3.1 Family

IND, GRP, FAM, COR. Age Range: 5 years and up.

Key Focus Areas: Family, social awareness, values, reciprocity, focus, communication.

(A) YOUR FAMILY, YOUR BASS

Discuss the different ways families support each other – remember to define family broadly.

Discuss the ways family members might hurt each other – be sensitive, as this could trigger traumatic memories. Healthy families care for and support each other – they form a stable support zone like the Bass note when we play music together.

Allocate each member of the group a family position (grandparents, parents, cousins, uncles, aunties, children) and a different rhythm part from the heartbeat rhythms (Section 10.9) for each. Then layer in a rhythm that connects each family member to the Bass note.

Reflect on what the Bass might represent in concrete terms – love, kindness, financial support, emotional support, etc. – things that stabilise the family unit and hold it together. Discuss the importance of connection in families and also the need for different family members to have some freedom to be themselves (have their own rhythm). What would this have sounded like if we all played the same part? Is any part of the family structure more important than another? If one part had stopped, would the others manage to continue? How is balance important in family relationships? How do different rhythms impact family relationships?

(B) SCRATCH MY BACK

Define the term 'scratch my back' in relation to the support we give to each other in healthy relationships. What are some of the ways we can support each other?

Explain that in this game you have to pass a scratch from your drum to another person as a way of saying that you would support them if they needed you.

Start with everyone playing the heartbeat foundation rhythm. Then choose one person to add the scratch to their rhythm and pass it over to someone else, using eye contact as a way of offering support to that person. The receiver then has to pass it on to another member in the same way, and so the game continues.

How important is it to share and support each other in families or as friends? What happens in families when people only think of themselves? Have you seen situations where one person is exploited by others – that is, they do all the work? If you were stuck in this sort of relationship, what could you do?

12.3.2 Me, Myself and I

IND, GRP, FAM. Age Range: 8 years and up.

Key Focus Areas: Self-awareness, emotional awareness, tolerance.

(A) MORE THAN A NAME

Ask people to think about the different things that make up someone's identity and list some broad categories, (e.g. appearance, culture, interests, social interests, values, etc.) on a white-board.

Explain to the group or the individual you are working with that you will all play a heartbeat rhythm on two beats of a four-beat measure. In the empty two beats between the Bass notes, one at a time each person will yell out one factor about themselves that corresponds to the category chosen by the facilitator.

In group situations people should take it in turn to yell out their contribution; in individual sessions the client and counsellor can swap turns. After each person has contributed, switch to a new category.

Have a discussion on the broad and shifting nature of identity, strengths, weaknesses and areas for growth.

(B) ZOMBIE

Discuss the different things and perspectives that make up a person's identity, for example culture, appearance, interests, family, friends, values and strengths. Write these on the white-board.

Start by enlarging the circle slightly.

One person should be picked as the zombie (start by asking people to put on their best zombie face and pick one person) and stand in the middle of the circle. They should choose a person, say their name and walk very slowly towards them (like a zombie – arms outstretched and with a weird face). Everyone should hit the Bass note in time with their steps (they must walk like a zombie, not run). The person being targeted must say one thing about their identity and the name of another person in the circle to avoid becoming a zombie themselves. If they are too slow, they can either join with or take the place of the person in the middle. If they say their trait and name someone else in time, the zombie must seek out the new person they have named, and so the game continues.

Note: This game can also be used to have people reflect on a wide range of issues in a fun way, including values, strengths, fears, emotions, boundaries, etc.

12.3.3 Friends

IND, GRP, FAM, COR. Age Range: 8 years and up.

Key Focus Areas: Healthy relationships, teamwork, social support, peer pressure, values.

(A) FRIENDS

Divide the group into pairs, or in one-to-one work team up with the person you are working with. Each pair must first agree on three different sounds to indicate direction or halt (see examples below).

One person should be blindfolded while the other holds a small drum – no talking is allowed. Enlarge the circle and create a series of obstacles in the middle of it (sometimes we use drums or people standing like pillars). The blindfolded person must walk to an object across the circle without hitting any of the obstacles. They should be supported by their friend walking just behind them, guiding them with their drum.

Common drum signals include:

- Bass – go straight.

- Tone – go sideways.

- Flam or Slap – STOP.

Discuss the role of friends in guiding each other through the obstacles of life. How important is it to have someone you trust in your life? What difference does it make to have help when you are faced with obstacles in your life (list some common obstacles). Connect this back to the values exercise 'What Does a Good Friend Do?' (Section 2.1). Is there someone you can help in this way?

(B) ARE YOU IN OR ARE YOU OUT?

In this game one person starts a rhythm and invites other individuals to join the rhythm through a nod of the head in their direction and mouthing the words 'come on in'. Each time a new person enters the rhythm, they can invite one other person to join with a nod (come on in) or exclude someone (stop playing) with a shake of their head (you can exclude an existing player or someone waiting to join). Each playing member can only invite or exclude one other member each.

How did it feel to be included or excluded? What sorts of things lead to people being excluded? How hard is it to be generous towards others and include them when others are excluding them? How easy is it to include those who are going through tough times? When you exclude someone, do you reveal something about yourself? Are there times it might be wise to exclude someone? How did including or excluding people impact the group as a whole?

12.3.4 Community

IND, GRP, FAM, COR. Age Range: 6 years and up.

Key Focus Areas: Social awareness, teamwork, communication, social confidence, social support.

(A) THE COMMUNITY CIRCLE

Discuss the different elements of community through the analogy of the drum-circle representing a community – explore:

- communication

- harmony

- diversity

- connection and belonging

- leadership.

Use the generic exercise 'Layering In, One Person at a Time' 16.4(a), a drum-circle exercise where one person starts a strong simple pulse and then each person enters one after the other with their own beat. Finish with a gradual 'fade away'.

Discuss how that particular example represented the factors above: Did we connect? Were we in harmony? Was there diversity and did it add to our output? Did we feel a sense of common purpose and connection? Why are these things so important? Did anything else come to mind?

(B) ONE FOR ALL, AND ALL FOR ONE

Teach the break – O,o,O-o O,o,O – representing the phrase 'One for all and all for one'.

Play a simple foundation rhythm or layer in an improvised rhythm and then include the break above. That is, count down and stop the rhythm and insert this phrase together before returning back to the rhythm – do this several times until it is tight.

1 + 2 + 3 + 4 +   1 + 2 + 3 + 4 +

O o O   o   O o O

Sometimes I get people to say the words over the top of the rhythm.

Discuss the type of support community members can offer each other, with a focus on your group as a community and the support they might offer each other outside the group session.

When we leave this group, how can we maintain the support for each other that we are giving here?

12.3.5 Diversity

IND, GRP, FAM, COR. Age Range: 6 years and up.

Key Focus Areas: Creativity, teamwork, communication, tolerance, respect.

(A) ADD YOUR RHYTHM

Divide the group into pairs and ask each group to come up with their own two-part pattern that fits the timing of a pulse that you will play in the background. Give them approximately five minutes to work out their duet.

Bring the players back into the circle and start the underlying pulse, then add in each pair gradually – each time a new pair comes in, lower the volume to receive them.

Discuss the nature of the rhythm as it changed with each new addition. How does diversity increase the richness of a community? What are some of the dangers of too much diversity?

How can we reduce such dangers? What allowed the rhythm to marry? How might this help people of different cultural backgrounds get on better together?

(B) IF WE WERE ALL THE SAME

Start by discussing a range of items and the implications if there was no diversity, (e.g. one type of tree, one type of car, one type of dress, one book, one type of food). Ask the group members to think of other things. What would it be like in a monoculture like this? What would we lose?

Start playing a standard 4/4 rhythm (no variation allowed). How quickly do you tire of this and begin to get frustrated? Mix it up with new patterns or improvisation and discuss the benefits of diversity

(C) UP AND DOWN

Use the 'Up and Down' exercise 12.2.6(a) but adapt the statements to explore individuality.

In many ways we are similar – we all seek love and wish to avoid suffering. We are each highly invested in our own lives. Examine the things that make us human, things that unite us and things that divide us. How can we reduce these divisions?

12.3.6 Culture

IND, GRP, FAM, COR. Age Range: 8 years and up.

Key Focus Areas: Values, connection and belonging, social awareness, tolerance, identity.

(A) FINDING FIVE

Use the 'Finding Five' 12.2.1(a) exercise and apply it to the concept of culture. On a white-board ask people to list things of value to their culture – if you have a multicultural group, you may end up with a broad list. Identify those values that are common across cultures.

(B) FIND YOUR WAY HOME

Use the 'Find Your Way Home' 12.2.10(c) exercise and connect the search for the empty chair to the search for what represents home – a place of belonging.

12.3.7 Country

IND, GRP, FAM. Age Range: 8 years and up.

Key Focus Areas: Regulation, belonging, identity, problem solving, teamwork, focus and attention.

(A) MINDFUL AWARENESS SCRIPT – COUNTRY

Warning: For some people the concept of country can evoke strong emotions – it can be useful to explore the concept of country through discussion before this exercise and monitor the group for any indications of distress.

Use a simple and very soft Bass pulse (40–60 bpm) or the Rhythmic Wave exercise (Chapter 11) as the focal point for this awareness exercise. Give instructions in a mellow, clear voice, speaking slowly in time to the rhythm. Remember, the script below is just a guide – make it your own.

- Relax your body.

- Adjust your body until you feel comfortable and relaxed. You may wish to close your eyes or focus your gaze on one spot. Focus on and relax any tension in your neck, shoulders, chest, arms, hands, back, hips, thighs, lower legs, feet.

- Slow your breathing, focus on your breath, becoming still.

- Now move that focus solely onto the sound of the Bass note.

- After a while, slowly transfer your focus to the concept of country – a place of belonging and connection.

- Breathe gently, slowly.

- Perhaps you might focus on a picture or memory of a place where you feel comfortable and at home. There is no right or wrong here – follow your thoughts until you settle on a place that evokes country for you.

- If unconnected thoughts enter your head, observe them dispassionately and bring yourself back to a picture or feeling of country.

- Try to notice the finer details of this picture you are developing – sounds, smells, objects, other people, etc.

- If other thoughts come into your mind, acknowledge them briefly and move your focus back to your place, your country

- Picture yourself now, in your country, observing the world around you, secure and grounded, connected to this place, solid in this place, belonging to this place.

- Move your thoughts slowly to these feelings secure – grounded, connected, solid, belonging.

- Breathe gently, slowly.

- Slowly move your focus back to the Bass note.

- Hold your focus on the Bass note as it slowly fades away.

If possible, sit in silence for 40–60 seconds; or if using the Rhythmic Wave exercise, you may like to rekindle the improvised rhythm that preceded this exercise.

(B) FIND YOUR WAY HOME

Use the 'Find Your Way Home' 12.2.10(c) exercise and connect the search for the empty chair to the search for what represents country – a place of belonging.

Discuss how it feels to be separated from a place of belonging and the different pathways to finding your way to your country if you are separated from it.

(C) FIND YOUR PLACE

Give each person in the circle a number in sequence. Say: 'Remember your number!'

Advise the group that once you start the game they need to remain silent (no talking or giggling). Choose one person to go into the middle and be blindfolded. Tell the person that the game starts when there is complete silence, as anyone talking will give the game away. The person in the middle has to find their seat by recognising the number of beats that correspond to the seated players' allocated numbers. Their chair will remain between the two numbers on either side of their given number.

Ask the group to move without changing the order of the sequence – in other words, they all stand and move a certain number of places in the same direction. The empty chair remains between the same two people, but in a new position in the circle.

Then the person in the middle should point in a direction. When they are pointed at, each person responds with the number of beats on their drum that represents their number – the person in the middle uses these signals to find their way back to their empty chair.

Rumble if you have ever felt lost or out of place? What helps you find your place when you feel lost? Can other people, friends and family help you find your place? How do the rhythms of your life impact your ability to find your place? How important is your own self-confidence in finding your place?

12.3.8 Survival

IND, GRP, FAM, COR. Age Range: 10 years and up.

Key Focus Areas: Creativity, problem solving, personal agency, self-belief, hope and positivity.

(A) CHANGE IS COMING

Discuss the nature of change as a constant in life and the need to adapt to change – find examples, such as change in climate, change in body, change in government, change in locality, change in workplace, change in schools.

In this exercise, the facilitator starts a rhythm and appoints a 'change maker' – this person can alter the rhythm in three different ways, by:

- changing the rhythm itself by adding or subtracting different beats

- changing the tempo by speeding up or slowing down

- changing the volume by getting louder or softer.

Other group members must adapt their rhythm in line with the change maker.

What helps you adapt to change? What are the consequences of not adapting? Is too much change unsettling or dangerous? Is leadership and communication important to implementing and adapting to change?

Note: This exercise also has strong application within corporate development programs.

(B) IF IT IS TO BE, THEN IT'S UP TO ME
This is an exercise that looks at behavioural change and self-responsibility.

Start with a discussion on power – how much power (agency) do you think you have to make the best of your life? How much power do you have over your thoughts and feelings? How much power do you have over how you act and the choices you make? What stops you from exerting that power? How can you gain the confidence and support to restore that power?

Note: It is important to acknowledge that people's feelings of agency vary at different times of their lives.

Once there is a consensus that in many ways we do have power to determine our future, and that we need to take responsibility for that (as much as we can), the phrase - O o O - o, O , B b B - b, B should be practised, which represents the theme 'If it is to be, then it's up to me.'

$$1 + 2 + 3 + 4 + \qquad\qquad 1 + 2 + 3 + 4 +$$
$$O o O \quad o \quad O \qquad\qquad B b B \quad b \quad B$$

A flowing rhythm should be played (which represents the flow of life) and the practitioner should tell the group that they will interrupt that flow with a count down of 4, 3, 2, 1, STOP, just like problems or challenges that surface from time to time in our own lives. To resume the flow, the group should play the break 'If it is to be, then it's up to me' (taking responsibility to find the solutions, make the right choices or seek help).

Finish by having everyone say the phrase over the top of the break.

(C) ACCENT THE POSITIVE

Use the Accent the Positive 12.2.3(a) exercise.

Discuss the importance of positivity, hope and self-belief for survival.

12.3.9 Growth

IND, GRP, FAM, COR. Age Range: 8 years and up.

Key Focus Areas: Self-awareness, hope, self-belief, goal-setting, relapse.

(A) GROW

In this game we play a double-time foundation rhythm slouched low in our seat, then on a signal we play that same tempo twice as fast again for 24 beats and raise our posture slightly before returning to the original tempo. This happens four or five times until we are standing fully upright and playing. Then the movement is reversed – each time getting lower and also quieter.

What are some of the things necessary for physical growth? What about psychological growth (maturity, wisdom)? Why would we need to keep growing in understanding as we age? What are some of the incentives to keep growing as you move through life? What are some of the dangers of standing still? What happens if you enter into a relationship where one person stops growing, or isn't interested in growing?

Note: This may not be suitable for aged care groups and those with physical disabilities.

(B) FROM LITTLE THINGS BIG THINGS GROW (USE TO EXPLORE GOAL SETTING)

One person should start a rhythm with one beat. Each subsequent person should layer in, adding one extra beat each to grow the rhythm. It is OK to stop and try out some different patterns before becoming fluid in the new rhythm, but each new rhythm should build on the rhythm that preceded it. The facilitator should keep track of the number of beats each time.

Discuss the way small steps can lead to great achievements, with relevance to personal growth. Use this exercise to look at 'goal setting' for an individual in relation to addressing a specific issue and moving forward in life.

Note how readily some people give up – discuss the importance of perseverance and taking time.

12.3.10 Responsibility

IND, GRP, FAM, COR. Age Range: 8 years and up.

Key Focus Areas: Social Responsibility, Social Awareness, Self-Awareness,

(A) ME, US AND THEM

This exercise looks at our responsibility towards others in our community.

In the middle of the circle put out a range of percussion instruments.

Explain to the group that you are all going to play a simple, stable rhythm together that represents the stability of your community (an analogy they may be familiar with by now). At any stage they can leave their chair, pick up a percussion instrument from the middle of the circle and play that instead of their drum for a while.

Explore what happens, in relation to the analogy of community:

- If everyone leaves the community at once to pick up percussion instruments, the rhythm changes, weakens, suffers, etc.

- The rhythm fails because everyone is too busy swapping instruments – no one takes responsibility.

- Certain people may act to hold the rhythm while others may experiment.

- The balance between the drums and percussion alters to the point of instability.

Note: This can be adapted for people with physical disabilities by having a choice of drum or percussion available to each person, without the need for them to leave their chair, and having people to assist them with swapping instruments if necessary.

(B) THE BLAME GAME

Key Focus Areas: Blame, self-responsibility.

Note: Don't mention the name of this game prior to playing it! It is important to get this introduction correct. In this game you will ask the group to work out the cause of people being eliminated from the rhythm. The aim of the game is not to stay in the rhythm but to work out why people are being eliminated.

Tell the group that you will stop the rhythm and one person will be told to stop playing – everyone has to guess who is to stop and why they were eliminated.

Stop the rhythm at any point and ask: 'Who is out and what's it all about?' People will yell different reasons, and as soon as someone blames somebody for doing something wrong, you will choose that person (the accuser) as the person to be eliminated without making it obvious why they were chosen.

Thus, the secret is that the first person to blame somebody else for something they apparently did wrong is the person eliminated. Resume the rhythm once somebody falls into this trap. It will generally take several goes before people realise it is 'blame' that is defeating them!

What are some of the ways blame defeats you in real life? How can you take responsibility for your life if you are always blaming others for what goes wrong? if you blame someone for something that happened to you, are you in effect saying they have the power to control your life? By avoiding blame, you take back that power.

12.4 Strengths and Virtues

Recognising and utilising one's strengths in order to get the most satisfaction from life is a core principal of Positive Psychology. These sessions cover a range of virtues, recognised in cultures across the world as being positive personality traits and which, when explored, can be used by individuals to improve their relationships, enhance their overall wellbeing and act to increase resilience in the face of adversity.

12.4.1 Courage

IND, GRP, FAM, COR. Age Range: 10 years and up.

Key Focus Areas: Values, self-awareness, risk taking, social support, self-belief, bullying.

(A) STANDING UP FOR IT

Ask each person to name one value they would be prepared to stand up for. The group should come up with examples – personal or public – of individuals who have stood up for this same cause.

Examples:

- Honesty – Would you stand up in the face of dishonesty? Can you give an example?

- Respect – Would you stand up in the face of disrespect? Can you give an example?

- Loyalty – Do you stand up for your friends or family? Can you give an example?

- Bullying – Would you stand up against a bully? Can you give an example?

Then, one at a time, each person asks the rest of the group a question, starting with the phrase 'Rumble if you'd stand up for...' and fills in the gap with something they think it is important to stand up for.

Discuss the challenges of courage. What is the difference between bravery and courage? Can you be brave and foolhardy at the same time? How can friends band together to be brave in numbers? Why are bullies cowards?

(B) INTO THE UNKNOWN

Each person should identify one activity they are fearful of doing from the list of activities below and then take a step into the unknown by giving it a go.

First, ask the group to acknowledge the feelings people go through when they enter into new challenges like this and provide emotional support. How do you provide emotional support for a friend who needs to be brave and take on a new challenge to move their life forward?

- Playing a solo.

- Dancing to the rhythm.

- Singing or rapping to the rhythm.

- Facilitating the rhythm.

- Beat-boxing.

Discuss the rewards of facing up to your fears and the importance of the emotional support from others in doing so.

(C) FEAR
Use the exercise 'Fear 16.1(g)' to examine the courage needed to overcome our fears

12.4.2 Honesty

IND, GRP, FAM, COR. Age Range: 8 years and up.

Key Focus Areas: Values, teamwork, social support, healthy relationships, peer pressure.

(A) TRUST ME
Ask people to voluntarily seek out another person to work with.

Prior to starting the exercise, the facilitator should remind the guide that they can either help or deceive their colleague in this exercise.

One person should be blindfolded in the middle of the circle and disorientated by rotating on the spot. They then have to find the one empty chair in the circle. They should choose a partner to be their guide, who can decide to either assist or undermine their search. Other people should swap places so that the blindfolded person is unaware of where the empty chair is situated. The guide uses their drum to indicate 'hot' or 'cold' as they get closer to the empty chair. Other members of the circle may tap their drum once to indicate if the person is getting too close to them.

Note: If the guide chooses to deceive the person in the middle, end the session after a couple of minutes.

Why did you choose the person as your partner? How much trust did you put in that person? How did it feel to be either supported or deceived? What is the connection between trust, friendship and our relationships in general. How important is trust in your relationships with other people? How hard is it to rebuild trust after it has been broken? Do you think most people are trustworthy? How can you protect yourself from those who are not?

Note: This may not be suitable for aged care and people with physical disabilities.

(B) TWISTING THE TRUTH AND THE SILENT LIE
Prior to starting one person should be secretly chosen to twist the truth. The facilitator should start with a simple pattern on their drum (representing the truth), which the group plays. The 'twister' changes that rhythm slightly by adding or dropping a note or two. Sometimes the new rhythm (a lie) may be taken up by others.

Why do we sometimes veer from the truth? How easy is it to lie in order to avoid problems? Do lies usually come back to haunt you? Where do lies sit in relation to your values? How easy is it to get caught up in a lie – do you have examples? What happens when we hear something untrue but don't say anything to challenge it?

(C) CROSSING THE LINE
USE TO EXAMINE BOUNDARIES
Ask every second drummer in the circle to move into the middle of the circle and then explain that there is an imaginary line down the middle and they need to stay on the correct side of that line (you could draw a line with chalk if necessary). Position them on one side of the line in a row, facing down the line, and have them make some jumps from one side of the imaginary line to the other (like jumping a skipping rope). Then pass out one bell to a member of the remaining drummers and explain that the signal for jumping across the line is when they hear the bell played three times in a row (demonstrate). If they miss the cue and fail to jump and are stuck on the wrong side, then they must re-join the drummers. Start a simple foundation rhythm and proceed.

Note: Occasionally play different bell patterns to test their listening skills.

Discuss the concept of 'crossing the line' or going too far (out on a limb). What are some examples of things you may have done or seen others do that 'crossed the line' (be careful to avoid blame and not to name people). What sorts of pressures make people do things that are cruel, dangerous, unwise or otherwise compromise their values? How can you stay on the right side of that line? How does crossing the line relate to honesty and our values?

Note: This may not be suitable for aged care and people with physical disabilities.

12.4.3 Perseverance – Sticking at It

IND, GRP, FAM, COR. Age Range: 8 years and up.

Key Focus Areas: Resilience, values, self-belief, social support.

(A) HANG ON IN THERE

The group should take on the challenge of rumbling for a set period or playing a more complex rhythm and maintaining it for a set period of time – start with one minute and work up.

Have a discussion exploring what gets in the way of persistence, the ease and consequences of quitting, and how the group members can support each other in persisting in the face of adversity. What are some of the areas in life where persistence is important? What are some of the consequences of giving up?

(B) QUITTING IS EASY

Teach a rhythm on the edge of the group's capacity – start slowly and speed up. Note that people can quit at any time, but there are rewards for persisting. Your persistence is often a measure of your faith in yourself.

How did persisting influence your success in this exercise? What are some of the rewards of persistence? How often do we walk away too early or too late? How do you know when to persist and when to walk away? In what situations in life might it be prudent to quit early?

12.4.4 Kindness

IND, GRP, FAM, COR. Age Range: 8 years and up.

Key Focus Areas: Empathy, social support, healthy relationships, communication.

(A) ARE YOU OK AND CAN I HELP?

Discuss the reciprocal nature of kindness. Call for examples where people have helped out a friend or stranger and examples of when they have been helped out by someone else.

In this exercise the break O o - O - o / o O - o - O represents the expression 'Are you OK and can I help?' When adding the drum break, people, if they choose, can voice this phrase in time with the rhythm. Practise this break several times.

1 + 2 + 3 + 4 +				1 + 2 + 3 + 4 +
Oo	O	o	o	O o O

Start by rehearsing one of the 4/4 rhythms from the rhythm catalogue (Section 10.9) and after each four measures add the break before re-entering the original rhythm.

Add a second part to the rhythm and have half the group play the original while the other half play part two. Then add the break on a regular basis.

Discuss different ways people can show kindness towards others and the way these acts can become part of the rhythm of our lives. Has anyone noted the infectious nature of kindness?

In relation to grief and loss, discuss how you can support people dealing with these experiences. What makes it hard to offer help to others? What makes it hard to ask for help when you need it?

(B) THE THOUGHTFUL RHYTHM

In this exercise the group should layer in one at a time with their own part, but prior to entering the rhythm they should be asked to be thoughtful of those still to come – this thoughtfulness comes in the form of:

- leaving space for others

- welcoming their contribution to the rhythm

- grounding them through the pulse if they get lost

- keeping the tempo stable

- encouraging them.

How important is it to be conscious of the needs of others when we live in communities? How does being thoughtful benefit us? What tends to reduce out thoughtfulness?

(C) PUT UPS – WHAT I LIKE ABOUT YOU

Use the 'Put Ups – What I Like About You' 12.2.6(b) exercise to examine kindness.

12.4.5 Teamwork

IND, GRP, FAM, COR. Age Range: 5 years and up.

Key Focus Areas: Coordination, teamwork, communication, cooperation, listening skills.

(A) ONE TO THE RIGHT, ONE TO THE LEFT

Bring the circle in tight so that each person's drum is close to those on either side. In individual work, sit opposite each other close together with the two drums touching on their outer rim.

1 + 2 + 3 + 4 +				1 + 2 + 3 + 4 +			
B	B	-	-	B	B	-	-
1 + 2 + 3 + 4 +				1 + 2 + 3 + 4 +			
B	B	O	-	B	B	o	-

Play the double heartbeat on your drum (BB--BB--), then add one Tone by hitting it on the drum of the person sitting to your right followed by the double Bass again on your own drum and one Tone on the drum of the person sitting on your left (BBO- BBo -). Go back to the heartbeat on your drum twice, then repeat. Call out the instructions:

- My drum.

- One to the right.

- My drum.

- One to the left.

Try different variations: two Tones (BBOO,BBoo) each side or three (BBOOO,BBooo), soft/loud, slower/faster. Always come back to your own drum for two sets of double heartbeats in between.

1 + 2 + 3 + 4 +	1 + 2 + 3 + 4 +
B B O O	B B o o

1 + 2 + 3 + 4 +	1 + 2 + 3 + 4 +
B B OOO	B B OOO

The instructions for two Tones would be:

- My drum.

- Two to the right.

- My drum.

- Two to the left.

1 + 2 + 3 + 4 +	1 + 2 + 3 + 4 +	1 + 2 + 3 + 4 +	1 + 2 + 3 + 4 +
B B O O	B B o o	O o O o O o O	O o O o O o O

Try this with the pattern two right, two left and two sets of five half notes on your own drum (BBOO,BBoo, OoOoO-OoOoO), using the instructions:

- My drum.

- Two to the right.

- My drum.

- Two to the left.

- My drum – five plus five.

Do this three times and then on the fourth time add two sets of three Flams (fl fl fl - fl fl fl-) instead of the five half notes – repeat at different tempos. Ask your participants to come up with their own patterns.

1 + 2 + 3 + 4 +				1 + 2 + 3 + 4 +		
fl	fl	fl	-	fl	fl	fl -

Discuss the cooperation required to do these exercises and the skills utilised, and how these apply to other teamwork situations. How important is communication and leadership to the success of this exercise?

Note: In individual therapy these exercises can be played between the drum of the counsellor and their client – instead of left and right, take it in turns to cross over onto your partner's drum.

(B) MARCO POLO

Note: This is not suitable for individuals.

First enlarge the circle. Then ask for a volunteer to be blindfolded in the middle of the circle. Place another individual or more (depending on the circle size) in the circle.

The blindfolded individual should try to find (touch) one other individual using the remaining drummers for support – they can provide clues on the target's whereabouts by signalling through their drums. Before starting, emphasise the teamwork required in this game between the drummers and between the drummers and blindfolded team member in the middle.

If the blindfolded person is getting a lot of confused signals, stop the game and address this issue, asking the drummers to try to work together to better inform the person in the middle.

Warning: Caution the blindfolded person about swinging their arms wildly.

Advanced: Instead of a rumble, the blindfolded individual calls out 'Marco' and the drummers adjacent to the people trying to escape in the middle of the circle reply with two tones (Polo).

Note: This may not be suitable for aged care and people with physical disabilities.

(C) ADDITIONAL EXERCISES FOR TEAMWORK

Use the additional teamwork exercises in Section 16.3.

12.4.6 Fairness

IND, GRP, FAM, COR. Age Range: 8 years and up.

Key Focus Areas: Social justice, resilience, positivity, emotional awareness, self-belief.

(A) IT'S UNFAIR!

Make a list on a white-board of one thing each person feels is unfair (try to be as specific as possible). Categorise them into different environments of:

- school/workplace

- family/home

- community/society.

Use the 'Rumble If You Hope to' 12.5.6(a) or 'Play How it Feels' 16.1(f) exercise to check in with the group on how these things impact them and follow with a discussion. The world is full of unfair situations – how reasonable is it to expect life to be fair? How can we move our world towards being a fairer place? Are we influenced by people who act fairly towards others? Do you always act fairly yourself? How do you deal with situations you think are unfair?

(B) DON'T LET IT BRING YOU DOWN

Ask one person to come up with an upbeat (positive) rhythm on their drum and then have the person sitting next to them play something downbeat (negative). Watch for changes in the emotional content of either player. Add additional players one at a time to increase the level of negativity and explore how this impacts the mood of the initial upbeat drummer.

How can you maintain your positivity in the face of others who may be cynical or angry?

These two approaches can also be played out between a counsellor and their client.

Adaption
Reverse the exercise so that one influences the other in a positive way – start off with a sad or despondent drummer and expose them to uplifting rhythms one at a time.

How does having positive people around you improve your situation? Are there some people you can't lift?

(C) BOUNCE BACK (BACK ON TRACK)
Use the 'Bounce Back (Back on Track)' 12.2.10(a) exercise to further explore how we can recover from injustice.

12.4.7 Forgiveness

IND, GRP, FAM, COR. Age Range: 8 years and up.

Key Focus Areas: Emotional awareness, emotional regulation, focus and attention, empathy.

(A) LET IT GO
THIS IS A GOOD ALTERNATIVE EXERCISE FOR FINISHING A SESSION

Discuss the dangers of not forgiving others or ourselves (e.g. a build up of negativity, loss of friendships, loss of trust and a focus on the past). Discuss the benefits of forgiveness (e.g. peace of mind, strength of character, release from the chains of resentment and anger and freedom to live in the present without the ties of the past holding you back). Discuss the obstacles to forgiveness.

Teach the following two parts.

1. O o O - O o B (It's your fault, it's my fault).

1 + 2 + 3 + 4 +   1 + 2 + 3 + 4 +

O o O -   O o B -

2. O o O - B - O - o - O - o - O (Let it all go and let's move forward).

1 + 2 + 3 + 4 +   1 + 2 + 3 + 4 +

OoO B - O   o O o O

Then start out with rhythm one and upon a signal, (4, 3, 2, 1), move to rhythm two.

Extension: Move from part one to improvisation and discuss how some patterns of resentment trap you and letting go of these brings back a lot of freedom.

(B) MINDFUL AWARENESS SCRIPT – FORGIVENESS

Examine the theme of forgiveness through discussion prior to this exercise (Chapter 11), with a focus on the healing power of forgiveness – forgiveness frees us from resentment, bitterness, anger and hurt. Forgiveness is about renewal. Forgiveness is something that we control, something we can take responsibility for – a power we alone can exercise.

Use a simple and very soft Bass pulse (40–60 bpm) or the Rhythmic Wave exercise (Chapter 11) as the focal point for this awareness exercise. Give instructions in a mellow, clear voice, speaking slowly in time to the rhythm. Remember, the script below is just a guide – make it your own.

- Relax your body.

- Adjust your body until you feel comfortable and relaxed. You may wish to close your eyes or focus your gaze on one spot. Focus on and relax any tension in your neck, shoulders, chest, arms, hands, back, hips, thighs, lower legs, feet.

- Slow your breathing – focus on your breath, aligning it to the pulse, and becoming still, breathe deeply and slowly.

- Now move your focus to the sound of the Bass note.

- Then slowly transfer your focus to the concept of forgiveness. Start by forgiving yourself, thinking about some of the mistakes you've made in your life. Acknowledge these while accepting that mistakes are part of life and that despite your mistakes you are still a valuable human being and you can be forgiven for these.

- Breathe gently and slowly, and in time with your breath say the words to yourself: 'I forgive myself.'

- Now move your thoughts to others who you feel have wronged you and extend your forgiveness to them individually.

- If other thoughts – perhaps resistance to or arguments against forgiveness – come into your mind, acknowledge them briefly and move your focus back to forgiving.

- Breathe gently and slowly, and in time with your breath make individual statements of forgiveness to those who you feel have hurt you.

- As you forgive them, imagine the negative feelings about them that you have harboured inside being released at the same time, leaving you free from resentment, anger and pain.

- Picture yourself now, free from the pain of the wrongs you have suffered at the hands of others, more welcoming and trusting and open to moving forward in your relationships.

- Breathe gently, slowly.

- Slowly move your focus back to the Bass note.

- Hold your focus on the Bass note as it slowly fades away.

If possible, sit in silence for 40–60 seconds, or if this is part of the Rhythmic Wave exercise, you may like to rebuild the improvised rhythm you started with.

Discuss the benefits of doing this exercise regularly.

(C) DROP IT
Use the 'Drop It' 12.2.5(e) exercise.

Explore this exercise in relation to forgiveness and dropping the resentment, anger and pain that are held inside us when we are unable to forgive.

12.4.8 Humour

IND, GRP, FAM, COR. Age Range: 5 years and up.

Key Focus Areas: Positivity, emotional awareness, social support, resilience.

(A) LAUGHTER IS CONTAGIOUS
ADAPTED FROM M. COLLARD
Bring the group in close and, if possible, arrange people so that each person leans towards the person on their right until their head rests on that person's shoulder (ensure people are comfortable with this form of contact). Then one person should start with the word 'ha' and each person should follow quickly with an additional 'ha' to the number the person before them voiced for example, ha, ha ha, ha ha ha, ha ha ha ha, ha ha ha ha ha. If someone gets it wrong or interrupts the sequence, you start again from the beginning.

The group should end up giggling.

How important is it to have someone in your life who can make you laugh? How important is it for you to see the lighter side of life? How easy is it for you to laugh at yourself? Why do we sometimes take pleasure in laughing at others, and is that OK?

(B) MAKE ME SMILE
Pair people up diagonally across the circle, with one person from each pair trying to make the other smile – the other should try to hold a blank expression. State the rules are no touching the person you are trying to amuse or leaving your seat.

Try it one pair at a time, with the remaining group members interpreting on their drums the emotions on the person's face as, or if, it changes.

Scientists have found that laughter is literally the best medicine and is essential for good health (Bennett and Lengacher 2008). When was the last time you had a good laugh? Could you help someone you know by making them laugh? Why do we take the world so seriously?

12.4.9 Humility

IND, GRP, FAM. Age Range: 8 years and up.

Key Focus Areas: Empathy, self-awareness, focus and attention, healthy relationships, regulation.

(A) THE EGO TRAP

Discuss how easy it is for pride to get in the way of humility. Being able to recognise the value and gifts of others, particularly when we are successful, is a fundamental aspect of humility, as is an understanding that no one individual is of more worth than another. Can you think of examples of successful people who have become arrogant?

In this game you should take one chair out of the circle and ask for a volunteer to stand in the middle. The group should play a foundation rhythm and the person in the middle can count the group down to STOP (4, 3, 2, 1, STOP). The same person (in the middle) should then do one of the following:

- Say out loud one character area they could do better in (e.g. 'I could be more generous.').

- Praise the character of another member (e.g. 'John is a generous person.').

Once this is done the person in the middle should restart the rhythm with the words 'One, two, let's all play' and pick a new member to stand in the circle, before returning to their vacated chair. The newly trapped group member should bring the group to a stop in the same way and so the game continues.

In individual work use the same countdown to stop the rhythm and take it in turns between the counsellor and the individual to talk about character traits they could work on to improve their character and the way they relate to others

– beware too much emphasis on the negative properties of an individual if they are already heavily self-critical.

Examine the pitfalls of ego and vanity and the importance of being humble and respecting others. What happens when people think they are better than others? What are the benefits of understanding your imperfections? Recognising our strenghts is an essential element in maintaining self-esteem – how does this impact our relationship with humility?

Note: This is adaptable for those with physical disabilities – instead of moving to the middle, participants should stay in their seats (don't remove a chair).

(B) MINDFUL AWARENESS SCRIPT – HUMILITY

Examine the theme of humility through discussion prior to this exercise, with a focus on humility as a precursor to self-improvement and wellbeing. Humility helps us understand, appreciate and respect others in all their imperfect permeations, reducing judgment and competitiveness between people. Humility also helps us overcome disappointments as we recognise our humanity and its accompanying imperfections.

Use a simple and very soft Bass pulse (40–60 bpm) or the Rhythmic Wave exercise (Chapter 11) as the focal point for this awareness exercise. Give instructions in a mellow, clear voice, speaking slowly in time to the rhythm. Remember, the script below is just a guide – make it your own.

- Relax your body.

- Adjust your body until you feel comfortable and relaxed. You may wish to close your eyes or focus your gaze on one spot. Focus on and relax any tension in your neck, shoulders, chest, arms, hands, back, hips, thighs, lower legs, feet.

- Slow your breathing – focus on your breath and align it to the pulse, becoming still.

- Now move your focus to the sound of the Bass note.

- Then slowly transfer your focus to the concept of humility – start with thinking about all that you have and giving thanks for that, even if it is just for the shoes on your feet. Understand that there are always people worse off than ourselves and that nothing happens in isolation; our luck is often at someone else's expense.

- Breathe gently, slowly and in time with the pulse, and give thanks to those people and things that support, reward and encourage you today.

- Now move your thoughts to recognising your own limitations and an understanding of the imperfections of life in general, and amongst life, all persons.

- If other thoughts – perhaps resistance to acknowledging others for your success or accepting your own weaknesses – come into your mind, acknowledge them briefly and move your focus back to the concept of humility.

- Breathe gently and slowly, and in time with your breath make individual statements of acceptance of your faults and imperfections.

- Now move your thoughts to the idea of ongoing learning – so much to learn and so many good teachers. Consider the concept of a student for life and every individual, no matter how meek or impoverished, you meet being a teacher with something worthy to impart to you.

- Picture yourself now, free from judging others or competing with others and instead being more accepting and appreciative of others and all their different strengths.

- Breathe gently, slowly.

- Slowly move your focus back to the Bass note.

- Hold your focus on the Bass note as it slowly fades away.

If possible, sit in silence for 40–60 seconds, or if this exercise is done as part of the Rhythmic Wave, you may wish to rebuild the improvised rhythm you started with.

Discuss the challenges of staying humble.

12.4.10 Gratitude

IND, GRP, FAM, COR. Age Range: 5 years and up.

(A) THE LOOKOUT

Play 'Musical Chairs' 12.6.6(b), but with each person moving one chair in a clockwise direction. Nominate the 'lookout chair'. It can be useful to make this chair a bit different – perhaps find a bigger, more stately chair.

Each time a new person reaches the lookout chair, they should nominate a set number of things (one to three) to be grateful for before the rhythm can resume.

Note: This exercise can be adapted for people with a physical disability by not moving but instead every chair becomes the lookout chair and each time you stop the rhythm a new person nominates the things they are grateful for.

How challenging is it to appreciate the positives in our lives? How can we change our focus away from needing more to accepting what we have? Does the company we keep influence our ability to do this? How is this related to balance?

(B) THE APPRECIATION CHAIR
ADAPTED FROM M. COLLARD

Play 'Musical Chairs' 12.6.6(b), with each person moving one chair in a clockwise direction. Nominate an 'appreciation chair'. It can be useful to make this chair a bit different – perhaps find a bigger, more stately chair, as in 'The Lookout' exercise above.

Each time a new person sits on this chair, the rest of the group should nominate a set number of things (one to three) that they appreciate about that individual before the rhythm continues.

Note: This exercise can be adapted for people with a physical disability by not moving chairs but instead every chair becomes an appreciation chair and each time you stop the rhythm you move one chair onwards from the previous recipient of praise.

When was the last time you told those closest to you how much you appreciate them? How easy is it to get into a rhythm of taking the individuals who support us most for granted? What gets in the way of being more openly grateful? In what other ways do you show your gratitude for others, other than in words?

12.5 Health and Wellbeing

This section focuses on a number of themes that impact our physical and psychological health.

In particular it deals with how we manage and recover from adversity, whether it be a relationship breakup, the death of a loved one or a descent into addiction. Two recurrent themes are focused upon in relation to recovery here: the importance of social support (healthy relationships) and the restorative power of acceptance and forgiveness.

The use of the mindful acceptance scripts are an important part of this series and should be practised regularly. The Rhythm2Recovery model adopts many of the principles of ACT that address the management of, and recovery from, painful and stressful life events through strategies, including mindfulness, that enlarge the capacity for acceptance of what is beyond one's control.

12.5.1 Relationships

IND, GRP, FAM, COR. Age Range: 8 years and up.

Key Focus Areas: Emotional awareness, teamwork, self-awareness, healthy relationships, values, communication.

(A) MOVE WITH ME

This exercise is done within a group in pairs or between a counsellor and their client.

Turn towards each other and place your palms together with only slight pressure at around shoulder height. Choose one person to lead and one to follow. The leader should move their hand slowly around the range of their arm extension while the follower maintains the same palm-to-palm contact (with the slight pressure required). Demonstrate if possible.

After a short period ask people to vary speed and then swap roles.

Discuss how it felt to lead and follow in this relationship and extend this concept into general or more intimate relationships. How did the pace of movement influence the connection? What about the consistency of the leader's movements? Did anyone lose contact? Why? How important was it to maintain some pressure? How does this connect to your experience of leading or following in relationships? Have you experienced relationships where you spent much of the time following or leading? How satisfying were these? How do we ensure balance in relationships?

Advanced

Get the group to pair up again and this time tell them to try not to have a leader but to flow together. Suggest they close their eyes if they like. Try this same exercise with no leader and follower – just using the tips of the fingers.

(B) RELATE TO THE RUMBLE

Issues Addressed: Clarification of relational values, shared experience.

Each person should think of something positive or negative that impacts their relationships. One at a time the group members should ask the group to 'rumble if…' they have shared a similar relational experience.

How do these factors connect to the values we discussed earlier? How easy is it to recover your relationship with somebody when these factors are present or your values are missing? Why do we compromise our values sometimes when it comes to our relationships? Who has done that? How well does that compromise serve us into the future?

12.5.2 Balance

IND, GRP, FAM, COR. Age Range: 8 years and up.

Key Focus Areas: Healthy relationships, teamwork, numeracy, focus, attention.

(A) IN BALANCE

Divide the group into two halves and pass out two parts to each half of the group (or between a counsellor and the individual they are working with) to be played in a sequence that balances the parts.

Timing	1 + 2 + 3 + 4 +	1 + 2 + 3 + 4 +
Part 1 Begins	B - B b	O o O -
Part 2 Answers	O o O -	O o O -
Part 1 Repeats	B - B b	O o O -
Part 2 Completes	O o O o	O - - -

Continue this four-part dialogue as a rhythm – lower the volume and ask people to focus on the balance between these parts and how they complement each other. Increase the speed and watch to see if the balance shifts. Then add a clap in the break at the end of the sequence.

Explore the different ways the two parts balance or complement each other and connect it to balance in life. What would happen if one half of the rhythm started to dominate the other? Who has had experiences like this where they were out of balance in a part of their life, or in a relationship? How do you get that balance back? Is it realistic to expect such balance? How does the pace of our lives impact the balance in our lives? What role did the clap play in balancing the two parts? How important is it to have some connection between the different elements of your life?

(B) COUNTING ON YOU
ADAPTED FROM K. S. MASALA/K. LADHA

Divide the group into two halves and tell them that the idea is to play eight Tone notes as a group in total (in time with the Bass pulse, which lies on the first note of every four beats – the first note of the bar), followed by an eight-beat break of silence and to continue this pattern. Practise this nice and slowly – four notes each (eight in total) until it flows easily.

Then stop and tell them that now every time they play, each half will have a different share of the eight notes. One half will start with seven and work down to one, while the other half will start with one and work up to seven, holding the eight-note silence between each change.

Allocate who starts with one and who starts with seven and proceed.

Note: For younger children I write the two parts in their seven different combinations on the white-board – this helps those less certain of their arithmetic.

Advanced

One half only plays Bass notes and the other half only plays Tones, and add tonal chimes (pentatonic scale) or other percussion instruments in the eight-note rest. This will require some false starts until people get the idea.

How much of getting the balance right in a relationship comes down to focused attention? How important is cooperation and collaboration in balanced relationships? Can you think of examples where people in relationships complement (balance) each other? What are the signs of a relationship that is out of balance?

12.5.3 Drugs and Alcohol

IND, GRP, FAM, COR. Age Range 8 years and up.

Key Focus Areas: Peer pressure, personal agency, self-belief, values, motivation, healthy relationships, social support.

(A) KEEP YOUR DISTANCE
Use the 'Keep Your Distance' 12.2.3(b) exercise.

Use this game to discuss the dangers that lead people to the problematic use of drugs and alcohol, particularly in relation to peer influence and which of those things we might reasonably be able to avoid.

(B) HOLD ONTO YOUR VALUES
Use the 'Hold Onto Your Values' 12.2.1(c) exercise.

Explore the role of values in identity and how these can be compromised by drug and alcohol use. Values give direction and meaning to our lives – when our values are strong, the influence of addiction is weakened.

(C) ARE YOU OK AND CAN I HELP?

Use the 'Are You OK and Can I Help?' 12.4.4(a) exercise to look at different ways people can support those impacted by addiction.

(D) MOTIVATIONAL EXERCISES

Use the exercises on motivation in Section 12.6.7 to examine what influences people to move away from problematic drug and alcohol use.

12.5.4 Grief

IND, GRP, FAM. Age Range: 8 years and up.

Key Focus Areas: Emotional awareness, self-awareness, social support, empathy, resilience.

(A) EMOTIONAL JOURNEY

When working with individuals the facilitator should ask the participant to play through the emotional content of a particular experience, memory or just a time period (e.g. the week since they last met). Say: 'Express this week on the drum, taking your time and using the drum as a safe and secure container into which you release these feelings. Avoid words.'

In groups, any individual can volunteer to play through their feelings on their drum in relation to a significant event in their lives, and the group may mirror that music in a show of empathy and support. There is no requirement to discuss the event at all. Ensure that the drummer plays slowly, so that people can follow.

How important is it to find constructive ways to release your feelings? Can sharing these with friends help? Many cultures move away from words to express feelings – why might that be? How important is it to have others recognise and empathise with your feelings?

Note: This exercise can bring up repressed emotion – ensure adequate support is available if required.

(B) THINKING OF YOU AND WHAT YOU'RE GOING THROUGH

Disappointment and sometimes real hardship are a part of life but can be tempered by the support we get from friends, family and sometimes complete strangers. Ask the group if anyone has a story of when someone has made them feel better by offering support and empathy after a disappointing or painful experience. If not, relate a story from your own experience. Ask if someone has an example of how they have supported a friend in a time of need. Define empathy. What are the rewards of helping others?

Say: 'In this exercise we are going to play a rhythm and add a rhythm break that represents the phrase "Thinking of you and what you're going through" – O o O - O - o O o - O - O – O.'

1 + 2 + 3 + 4 +	1 + 2 + 3 + 4 +
OoO o	OoO o O

Practise this sequence as a group a number of times and then insert it as a break into a simple rhythm from the rhythm catalogue (Chapter 10). Say: 'We will start a rhythm and count down to stop – instead of stopping, we will add this break and then return back to the rhythm on its completion. As we play, think about someone who might benefit from your support.' Demonstrate.

Discuss the importance of support from others when you are feeling low and how similarly you can offer support to your friends at these times. What avenues can you turn to if you can't find support from friends or family? How does this type of support relate to our responsibilities within our community? How much support can you offer without compromising your own health or safety?

(C) ARE YOU OK AND CAN I HELP?

Use the 'Are You OK and Can I Help?' 12.4.4(a) exercise.

Explore different issues around supporting others in time of grief.

12.5.5 Healing

IND, GRP, FAM. Age Range: 10 years and up.

Key Focus Areas: Resilience, self-belief, self-awareness, regulation, emotional awareness, problem solving, creativity, social support, acceptance.

(A) IT TAKES TIME

This exercise looks at the challenges of reconnection after trauma or loss. The group is told that on a given signal from the facilitator they are to stop playing and rumble. The facilitator keeps playing but changes to a different rhythm (slightly more complex). The group then has to try to reconnect with the new rhythm; repeat several times.

What helped you reconnect in this exercise? When life throws challenges at you, how hard is it to pick up the pieces and get on with your life? What can help you do this? What gets in the way? How important is patience in this situation? How important is group support?

(B) HELP ME OUT, IF YOU CAN

Use the 'Help Me Out, If You Can' 12.2.8(c) exercise.

Examine the challenges of asking for support in times of grief.

(C) MINDFUL AWARENESS SCRIPT – ACCEPTANCE

Examine the theme of acceptance in relation to grief and loss through discussion prior to this exercise, with a focus on validating the feelings that arise when we are experiencing these events. Accepting our feelings and the accompanying hurt, sensations and confusion allows us to avoid getting overrun by them.

Use a simple and very soft Bass pulse (40–60 bpm) or the Rhythmic Wave exercise (Chapter 11) as the focal point for this awareness exercise. Give instructions in a mellow, clear voice, speaking slowly in time to the rhythm. Remember, the script below is just a guide – make it your own.

- Relax your body.

- Adjust your body until you feel comfortable and relaxed. You may wish to close your eyes or focus your gaze on one spot. Focus on and relax any tension in your neck, shoulders, chest, arms, hands, back, hips, thighs, lower legs, feet.

- Slow your breathing – focus on your breath, aligning it to the pulse, becoming still.

- Now move your focus to the sound of the Bass note.

- Then slowly transfer your focus back to your body and those parts where you may be feeling sensations – observe any bodily feelings, tingling, warmth, etc. with curiosity and interest, like an explorer or birdwatcher. Focus closely on these sensations in all their different states, letting any other thoughts that come to mind pass gently by.

- Breathe gently, slowly and in time with the pulse.

- As you breathe and focus on these feelings, try to make some space for them, allowing them just to be there – breathe in and around them. Maintain your focus on these feelings but see them from a detached perspective, where you control the view.

- Breathe gently and slowly, and in time with your breath make individual statements of acceptance of your feelings and sensations – these are normal.

- Now move your thoughts to the idea of acceptance, allowing a warmth to settle over these feelings. A warmth of understanding, even to those feelings of angst, pain or distress – breathe.

- Picture yourself now, free from the dominance of these feelings and instead more accepting and appreciative of them – they have a right to exist and be a part of you without overshadowing or dominating you.

- Breathe gently, slowly.

- Slowly move your focus back to the Bass note.

- Hold your focus on the Bass note as it slowly fades away.

If possible, sit in silence for 40–60 seconds, or if doing this as part of the Rhythmic Wave exercise, you may prefer to rebuild the rhythm you were playing in the beginning.

Discuss the challenges and benefits of acceptance.

12.5.6 Hope

IND, GRP, FAM, COR. Age Range: 6 years and up.

Key Focus Areas: Positivity, self-belief, social support.

(A) RUMBLE IF YOU HOPE TO

Issues Addressed: Universality, goal setting.

Each person should nominate something they 'hope to' achieve in the future and ask the rest of the group to rumble if that is also on their 'hope list'. After each rumble the facilitator should write these aspirations on a white-board opposite the name of the person who raised it.

For example: rumble if you hope to find a soul-mate one day; rumble if you hope to have a stable job one day; rumble if you hope to get your life back on track one day.

Discuss areas of commonality in our hopes and dreams, as well as the importance of hope in achieving them. How important is it to have realistic ambitions? How can you design a pathway of small steps to reach your goals? How can you enlist support to help you achieve your goals? Are your goals selfish or for the greater good?

(B) THE GIFT OF HOPE

Issues Addressed: Self-belief, reinforcement of individual capacity.

For this exercise use the aspirations from the 'Rumble If You Hope To' exercise above, where each person has described a dream for the future and had it written on the white-board.

Ask each member to pick one of the aspirations of their colleagues (from the list on the white-board) and nominate one reason (stemming from a strength) why they see that potentially happening for that person. Younger people may simply say: 'I hope you get what you dream of because...'

Explore the ways we can engender hope in our friends when they may be losing hope, and how important that may be. What difference does it make having someone to affirm your dreams or ambition? How can we best support those close to us to realise their hopes?

12.5.7 Belonging

IND, GRP, FAM, COR. Age Range: 6 years and up.

Key Focus Areas: Identity, acceptance, connection, values, awareness, focus, healthy relationships, creativity, problem solving, social awareness, regulation.

(A) FIND YOUR BASS – FIND YOUR PLACE

Give individuals or groups a rhythm each that is in four time, within their capacity and critically has a Bass note as the first note of the bar.

Start a rhythm and ask them to come in at their leisure by joining their Bass note to yours.

Discuss what that Bass note might represent in terms of things that help connect people together in healthy ways and things that provide you with a sense of solidarity and grounding. List these points of connection on a white-board. How important is recognition and acceptance to your feeling of belonging?

After this discussion introduce a four Bass note break (B - - - B - - - B - - - B - - -) That is, count down the rhythm to stop and hit the Bass note four times (to represent four central values or foundations in your life), before returning to the rhythm.

1 + 2 + 3 + 4 +	1 + 2 + 3 + 4 +	1 + 2 + 3 + 4 +	1 + 2 + 3 + 4 +
B - - -	B - - -	B - - -	B - - -

Extension: Agree on four central values or foundations that provide a sense of stability in times of uncertainty. Write these down on a white-board.

Whenever the break is played, the group yells out these elements between each of the four Bass notes.

(B) LISTEN FOR THE BASS

In the Rhythm2Recovery model, the Bass note is the home note – a place of connection and belonging. Ask your participant/s to discuss this concept – where do they call home? What does it mean to belong?

Do a call and response with a focus on the Bass, for example say: 'If I play a Bass note then no echo, reply with a five Bass rumble.'

Discuss how having a place of belonging, and recognising it, provides us with a platform of stability and safety for when other aspects of our lives become challenging. This same platform provides us with a launching pad for new directions and opportunities. A first step in meeting the challenges of life is establishing a secure Base!

(C) FIND YOUR PLACE

Use the 'Find Your Place' 12.3.7(c) exercise to further examine belonging.

(D) LAYER IN YOUR RHYTHM

Each member should add their own rhythm to the mix one at a time. This exercise can be used to:

- showcase the importance of diversity in enriching community

- explore the different elements required in finding harmony with others in society

- examine the issues of connection and acceptance that provide people with a sense of belonging.

How easy is it to connect with others if your rhythm is running too fast? Can you see that timing impacts connection? If you are struggling to connect with others, how important is it to be prepared to change? What things might help you find a better rhythm so that you can meet people and find harmony with them?

12.5.8 Acceptance

IND, GRP, FAM, COR. Age Range: 8 years and up.

Key Focus Areas: Resilience, self-belief, coordination, teamwork, positivity, self-awareness.

(A) STRUGGLE STOP

In this game, the group rotates in one direction, with two chairs on opposite ends of the circle nominated as 'Struggle Stop' and 'Struggle Start'. Identify everyone's dominant (strong) hand and have them recognise when they reach the 'Struggle Start' chair that they must play with their non-dominant hand; when they reach the 'Struggle Stop' chair, they can revert back to their dominant hand. So at any one time, half the group is struggling with their weaker hand while the other half is managing OK, drumming with their strong hand. Advise them that they have the option to just hit the Bass note if they feel they are losing their way in 'Struggle territory'.

Begin a one-handed rhythm, with half the group playing with their 'strong' hand and half with their 'weaker' hand, depending on where they are sitting in relation to the two nominated chairs. Make sure the rhythm isn't too hard or too easy; B – O – B B O O works well. Vary the tempo to get the right level of difficulty – playing it with your non-dominant hand should be a struggle! Rotate seats using a drum-call or countdown, with each person in the 'Struggle Start' half playing with their weaker hand and continuing to do so until they reach the 'Struggle Stop' chair. Swap regularly so that each person gets a chance to experience the different sides.

1 + 2 + 3 + 4 +	1 + 2 + 3 + 4 +
B - O -	B B O O

What did it feel like when you were struggling with your weaker arm? Did you feel unconnected? Did anyone give up the struggle and just hit the Bass? How different was it when you gave up the struggle? Are there areas in your life that you are always struggling with? How hard would it be to accept these and give up fighting against them? Does giving up the struggle mean you can't change things? Acceptance is not necessarily resignation. How can we recognise what is worth the struggle and what might be better approached in a more passive way?

(B) FIND YOUR STRENGTHS RHYTHM GAME

Ask each person to think about one of the core strengths (things that they do well). List these on a white-board. Play a 4/4 rhythm of your choice and teach the group how to count down to a break of B - B - Bb -- (4, 3, 2, 1, B-B-Bb--. There is a one-count rest after the final Bass note before the rhythm resumes.

1 + 2 + 3 + 4 +   1 + 2 + 3 + 4 +

B - b -   B b Shout out

Have each participant count down the rhythm one at a time and in this final gap have the participants shout out their signature strength, before the group resumes the rhythm. Finish with everyone yelling their strength word together in that gap.

Examples of Core Strengths (Adapted from M. Seligman 2002)

Curiosity	Love of learning	Open mindedness
Street smart practicality	Social and emotional intelligence	Seeing the big picture
Courage and bravery	Perseverance	Kindness and generosity
Teamwork and loyalty	Fairness	Leadership
Humility	Creativity	Gratitude
Forgiveness	Optimism	Humour and playfulness

How aware are you of the things you do well (your strengths)? How might you use your strengths to move your life forward? Can you think of other exceptional people who have the same strengths as you? How can you use an awareness of your strengths to build up your less-developed aptitudes? How might focusing more on the strengths of others improve your relationships.

(C) DROP IT

Use the 'Drop It' 12.2.5(e) exercise to explore letting go of those factors, thoughts, feelings, etc. that are negatively impacting your psycho-social health.

12.5.9 Love

IND, GRP, FAM. Age Range: 8 years and up.

Key Focus Areas: Focus and attention, regulation, social awareness, healthy relationships, self-awareness, empathy, social support, values.

(A) MINDFUL AWARENESS SCRIPT – LOVE

Prior to this exercise, examine the theme of love in relation to your relationships and the care you offer to others and have experienced in return. Focus on the power of love to heal wounds, overcome disagreements and reconnect people who may be lost and alone. Focus on love as a strength – a powerful radiant light that penetrates the darkness in our lives and in our world.

Use a simple and very soft Bass pulse (40–60 bpm) or the Rhythmic Wave exercise (Chapter 11) as the focal point for this awareness exercise. Give instructions in a mellow, clear voice, speaking slowly in time to the rhythm. Remember, the script below is just a guide – make it your own.

- Relax your body.

- Adjust your body until you feel comfortable and relaxed. You may wish to close your eyes or focus your gaze on one spot. Focus on and relax any tension in your neck, shoulders, chest, arms, hands, back, hips, thighs, lower legs, feet.

- Slow your breathing – focus on your breath and try to align it to the pulse, becoming still, breathing deeply and slowly.

- Now turn your focus to the sound of the Bass note and maintain the alignment of your breath to the pulse.

- Then slowly bring your focus to the concept of love – look deep inside you and see if you can feel a sensation of warmth that you recognise as love. Perhaps you feel the presence of warmth in your body, a warm light within you. If you like, you may place a hand on your heart and feel the warmth of that loving energy as it grows within you. Focus on this warmth, this light, this feeling of positive intent towards yourself and others.

- Keep breathing gently, slowly and in time with the pulse.

- As you breathe, focus on extending these feelings outward towards others you respect and value, imagining this warmth and light moving from you and enveloping those you care for.

- Continue to breathe gently and slowly, and in time with your breath make individual statements of love towards yourself, other people you care for and, if possible, those who have wronged you. Share your love as widely as possible, perhaps encompassing all living things.

- If other thoughts move into your mind, recognise them and allow them to drift on by as you resume your focus on love.

- Now move your thoughts to the idea of receiving love. Imagine the same warmth you shared with others returning to you now, from them and others, settling into your body with feelings of peace and ease. Let these warm and comfortable feelings seep into your deepest being – breathe.

- Breathe gently, slowly.

- Slowly move your focus back to the Bass note.

- Hold your focus on the Bass note as it slowly fades away.

If possible, sit in silence for 40–60 seconds; or if you are doing this exercise combined with the Rhythmic Wave exercise, you may like to resume the improvised rhythm you started with.

Discuss the meaning of love and the importance of love for self and others.

(B) WHAT I'D DO FOR LOVE

The facilitator should pose a number of questions beginning and ending with the phrase: 'Rumble if you would…for love.' Fill in the gaps with:

- risk your life

- give away all your dreams

- move to another town

- move to another country

- leave behind your friends

- leave behind your family

- steal

- hurt another

- compromise your values.

Ask your participants to come up with their own statements.

Discuss the dangers of unconditional love.

(C) NOBODY LOVES YOU WHEN YOU'RE DOWN AND OUT

First make a list on the white-board of the sorts of things that ostracise people or lead to setbacks in their lives – they can be drawn from real experiences.

Take every second person out of the circle and have them sit down in the middle of the circle (creating a mini circle themselves, with each person facing their empty chair).

Showcase the 4/4 rhythm B b O o. Explain to the group that you will all play this rhythm and count down to STOP (4, 3, 2, 1, STOP). In the gap the people on each side of an empty chair can choose to love them or leave them by playing either the Tone three times (leave them – they stay down and out) or the Bass three times (love them – they return) in the gap before you all return to the rhythm. But both players (either side of the empty chair) must play the three Basses if the person is to return and they can't communicate their intentions with each other. If only one plays the Basses and the other plays Tones, the person stays down and out.

$$1 + 2 + 3 + 4 +$$

$$B \quad b \quad O \quad o$$

Start the rhythm and go in one direction, focusing on one empty chair at a time (i.e. each time you STOP, only the players on either side of the empty chair can respond).

How did it feel to be down and out in the middle? Did having others with you make a difference? How did it feel to be welcomed back? What about the feeling of being denied back? How hard is it to be generous to others when they are down on their luck? What gets in the way?

12.5.10 Death

IND, GRP, FAM. Age Range: 10 years and up.

Key Focus Areas: Empathy, social support, resilience, emotional awareness, regulation, focus, attention.

(A) THE ECHO WAVE
Use the 'The Echo Wave' 12.2.5(d) exercise.

Explore the finite nature of things and the cycle of life and death.

(B) ARE YOU OK AND CAN I HELP?
Use the 'Are You OK and Can I Help?' 12.4.4(a) exercise.

Examine the support we can offer people who are dealing with the loss of a loved one.

(C) MINDFUL AWARENESS SCRIPT – DEATH

Age Range: 15 years and up.

Note: This mindful script focuses on an area that some may find contentious and that may give rise to strong emotions – I always make the mindfulness session voluntary but conduct the opening discussion with the whole group. For younger participants, permission should always be obtained from parents and guardians prior to beginning this exercise and post-support services should be available if required.

Examine the theme of death in relation to rhythm and the cyclical nature of life. Death is an experience all of us will face at some stage, as it is an essential component of life – the two are inextricably linked. Different cultures deal with death in different ways, as do different individuals – some are less able to accept death than others. Being aware of the inevitability of death allows us to appreciate the privilege of life and those we care for. It allows us to understand the passing of those we love, even as we struggle through the grief and pain of that loss. And it maintains our connection to the realities of our lives within the natural world.

Use a simple and very soft Bass pulse (40–60 bpm) or the Rhythmic Wave exercise (Chapter 11) as the focal point for this awareness exercise. Give instructions in a mellow, clear voice, speaking slowly in time to the rhythm.

- Relax your body.

- Adjust your body until you feel comfortable and relaxed. You may wish to close your eyes or focus your gaze on one spot. Focus on and relax any tension in your neck, shoulders, chest, arms, hands, back, hips, thighs, lower legs, feet.

- Slow your breathing – focus on the breath, in and out.

- Now move your focus to the sound of the Bass note and align your breath to the pulse. Becoming still, breathe deeply and slowly.

- Then slowly bring your focus to the concept of death: the passing of life as part of the natural sequence of life; death as a reminder of the impermanence of all things; death as a reminder of the vitality of life and all its value.

- Keep breathing gently, slowly and in time with the pulse.

- You may find images or thoughts appearing of those you have loved who have died and for whom you still grieve. Feelings may arise out of your grief – allow those thoughts, visions and feelings to come, acknowledge them, make room for them and return your focus to your breath.

- Breathe.

- As you breathe, use the cycle of your breath to reinforce this notion of the ongoing, inevitability of the life-and-death cycle – death as a natural part of life.

- Remind yourself of life – how the vitality of life stands in contrast to the stillness of death. Let death remind you of the value of life, your life and the lives of others.

- Continue to breathe gently and slowly, and in time with your breath make individual statements of love towards those you may know who have passed from this life.

- If other thoughts move into your mind, recognise them and allow them to drift on by as you resume your focus on the breath. The breath as a reflection of life and death – the cycle of life and death, life begetting death and death begetting life.

- Breathe gently, slowly.

- Slowly move your focus back to the Bass note.

- Hold your focus on the Bass note as it slowly fades away.

If possible, sit in silence for 40–60 seconds.

Ask the group for any thoughts or feelings that have arisen from that session. Provide follow-up support for any individual who may require it.

12.6 Families, Teams and Communities

This section has been designed to cover topics central to families, teams (including corporate management) and larger community organisations. It has a strong focus on communication and other areas of inter-personal relationships, including power dynamics. Understanding the central relationship between individual life satisfaction and social connection highlights the critical importance of these sessions. Teamwork is a central theme of all the relational discourses in the Rhythm2Recovery model, and the group exercises described here allow for a useful examination of participants' collaborative skills.

Note: Although some of these exercises can be adapted for individuals, most are better suited to groups.

12.6.1 Leadership

IND, GRP, FAM, COR. Age Range: 6 years and up.

Key Focus Areas: Teamwork, communication, healthy relationships, self-awareness, social awareness.

(A) THE HUMAN MAZE

Issues Addressed: Teamwork, leadership, trust and guidance.

Place four or five people in random positions in the circle – ask them to stand as pillars, with their hands to their sides and no movement.
   One person should be blindfolded and then has to pass through the human maze with assistance from the remaining drummers, who indicate the direction of movement by signalling on their drums – using their sound to attract the maze runner in their direction.

Note: It may be necessary to stop the process if the blindfolded person is getting confusing messages from the drummers, reinforcing the need for them to work together to improve their communication.

Modification
You can also add a clear signal (e.g. Flam) for STOP.

What helped guide the subject through the maze? What hindered that guidance? How easy was it to trust the directions given by the drummers? Were you aware of a leader amongst the drummers or did they work well as a team to guide you?

Note: This may not be suitable for aged care or people with physical disabilities.

(B) STOP CUT

Issues Addressed: Leadership, communication, consultation.

Teach the basics of a 'stop cut' and 'back to play' – two drum-circle facilitation techniques (see Section 7.1). Model this with the group a few times and then invite participants one at a time to stop the group using a 'stop cut' and restart it using '1, 2 let's all play'.

Discuss what worked or didn't and why – how do these issues relate to leadership? How important is clear communication from a leader?

(C) FIND YOUR STRENGTHS

Use the 'Find Your Strengths' 12.5.8(b) exercise.

Examine strengths in relation to effective leadership.

12.6.2 Communication

IND, GRP, FAM, COR. Age Range: 5 years and up.

Key Focus Areas: Listening skills, focus and attention, healthy relationships.

(A) CALL AND RESPONSE

Use the 'Call and Response' 12.1.1(a) exercise.

Examine this exercise in relation to effective communication. In particular, explore how timing impacts effective communication. How often does poor timing get in the way of good communication?

(B) ATTENTION

Specialist Population: Sensory perception disorders.

Showcase two short rhythm phrases and then show the group the two specific responses required each time they hear these two rhythms.

Play 'Call and Response' 12.1.1(a) and occasionally include these two rhythm phrases, which people must listen out for and respond differently to. Each time they hear the chosen rhythms they must respond with either of the following:

- Rhythm 1 – silence

- Rhythm 2 – brief rumble.

Note: Use volume changes to make it more challenging – bring the volume right down.

Discuss how easy it was to react to the different signals (warnings) and not get caught in the flow of responding automatically the same way each time. What else can lessen your ability to listen well to others? Are there patterns in your listening and responding that undermine your communication with others? What are some of those patterns you need to be alert to?

(C) LISTEN CLOSELY

Use tonal chimes (pentatonic scale, CDEGA), or any other resonating instrument (the longer the resonance the better), and play one note each around the circle – don't initially ask for people to wait for the resonance to stop but each time ask them to listen more closely before coming in. See how long it takes before they are listening to the full resonance.

Discuss the challenges of listening well. What gets in the way (barriers) and what helps, and how does this impact relationships? Who here feels they are not listened to well by other people around them? Who here has been found guilty of not listening well to other people? What are some of the consequences of poor listening skills? What are some of the skills of good listening? How can mindfulness help improve our listening skills?

12.6.3 Power Dynamics

IND, FAM, GRP, COR. Age Range: 6 years and up.

Key Focus Areas: Healthy relationships, bullying, personal agency, self-confidence.

(A) THE CONTROLLER
ADAPTED FROM C. SLOTOROFF

Issues Addressed: Power dynamics, controlling relationships, frustration, patience, acceptance.

Choose one person in the group as the controller – the controller can denote who plays and who doesn't. (In individual sessions the counsellor takes on this role.)

Agree as a group on two signals – one for PLAY and one for STOP. The controller can direct the entire group or an individual.

The rules are firm – you may only play at the invitation of the controller and must stop playing when they ask you to.

The controller should either begin a rhythm or ask someone to begin and the exercise extends from there, with people being directed to start or stop at the whim of the controller.

What did it feel like to be controlled like that by somebody else? Were there feelings of resentment towards the controller? Did you find yourself becoming frustrated? Can you recall other situations where you were at the mercy of others' power (be sensitive here)? How healthy is it when one person exercises complete power over another? When might it be acceptable? When do you think it might be destructive? In situations where you know you have no power (e.g. say when you are stuck in traffic), how important is patience? What about acceptance – how can developing patience and acceptance improve your outcomes in situations like these?

(B) I'VE GOT THE POWER

Draw up a list of situations where people feel powerless and write these on a white-board. Then brain-storm how people can manage these situations and regain their sense of control.

Examples:

- Powerless to stop my partner's drinking – put in a boundary that I will not remain in the same space if they drink.

- Powerless to stop my parents from putting me down – spend more time with friends who lift me up.

- Powerless to stop the bullying that I suffer at school/work each day – ask a friend to record the bullying behaviour on their phone and report it.

Teach the rhythm phrase Bo - Bo - B (I've - got the Pow-er). Practise playing this rhythm three times, followed by three Flams – fl, fl, fl (Yes I have).

1 + 2 + 3 + 4 +   1 + 2 + 3 + 4 +

B o B o   B fl fl fl

The group should play a 4/4 rhythm from the rhythm catalogue (Chapter 10) and at any time an individual can play the rhythm break above over the top of the rhythm. On hearing the break the group should stop the rhythm and answer the third call with the three Flams before returning to the rhythm.

Demonstrate this once before beginning the exercise.

Finish with everyone doing and saying the break together.

Remind people that there are usually ways for them to regain power, in situations like those we have discussed, if they are patient, creative and enlist the support of trusted friends.

12.6.4 Values

IND, GRP, FAM, COR. Age Range: 6 years and up.

Key Focus Areas: Self-awareness, identity, peer pressure, values, relationships, meaning.

(A) THE VALUES RHYTHM
Use the 'The Values Rhythm' 12.2.1(b) exercise.

(B) HOLD ONTO YOUR VALUES
Use the 'Hold Onto Your Values' 12.2.1(c) exercise.

(C) FINDING FIVE

Use the 'Finding Five' 12.2.1(a) exercise.

See also Section 2.1.

(D) CROSSING THE LINE

Use the 'Crossing the Line' 12.4.2 exercise.

12.6.5 Creativity

IND, GRP, FAM, COR. Age Range: 8 years and up.

Key Focus Areas: Problem solving, collaboration, communication.

(A) FIND YOUR VOICE

Using the universal heartbeat rhythm as a back-beat, participants should come up with a short, two-phrase Rap rhyme (e.g. 'When I'm low, I've got no flow/ And all my friends don't wanna know') to punctuate the four-beat silence in between the Bass pulse.

Space out the heartbeat rhythm and showcase examples: BB 'Feel the beat', 'Move your feet', BB 'Say it loud', 'Say it proud' BB, etc.

1 + 2 + 3 + 4 +	1 + 2 + 3 + 4 +	1 + 2 + 3 + 4 +	1 + 2 + 3 + 4 +
B B Feel the beat	B B Move your feet	B B Say it loud	B B Say it proud

Give a theme for the lyrics (e.g. self-belief/ survival/ friendship/ recovery, etc.) and then ask people to go away in small groups or pairs, and come back with two or more lines for the song. Each member of the group should sing one line or they can sing their lines together. Start the pulse (BB - -) and layer in each vocal part around the circle one at a time – if it is sounding good, repeat or try stopping again and developing a group chorus.

1 + 2 + 3 + 4 +

B   B   -   -

Adaption

You can space the pulse out to eight beats and extend the verses to four lines.

Add different RAP moves to emphasise the lyric.

Discuss the way music impacts people's lives and the way lyrics can inspire the best from people and lead to social change.

(B) MAKE UP YOUR OWN

Each person should come up with their own rhythm – give people around five minutes to find this and allow them to move away from other people to get some creative space.

Each individual should teach their rhythm to the other participants, who then play it as a group. In individual work, the individual should teach their counsellor.

Try to find two parts from two different group members that might work together, and divide the group into two parts to play these. Or in individual work, the practitioner should combine a rhythm of their own with that of the person they are working with and both play together, exchanging parts.

Discuss the importance of creativity and problem solving in addressing life's challenges – seek examples of this, such as individuals surviving being lost in the wilderness or the global response to increasing carbon emissions. If appropriate, extend this discussion into helping address the personal challenges relevant to the individuals you are working with. How important was your level of confidence in succeeding in this exercise? Would it have been easier for you working with someone as a creative team?

12.6.6 Change

IND, GRP, FAM, COR. Age Range: 8 years and up.

Key Focus Areas: Adaption, creativity, positivity, social support, problem solving, awareness, self-belief.

(A) CHANGE IS COMING

Use the 'Change Is Coming' 12.3.8(a) exercise.

Explore the different aspects of managing and leading change.

(B) MUSICAL CHAIRS VERSION 1

Issues Addressed: Change and perspective.

Place a percussion instrument on every second chair. Practise a signal for stopping the group and holding silence across seven counts before re-entering the rhythm (i.e. stopping on the first note of a four-count bar and coming back on the first note of the second bar following that – STOP, 2, 3, 4, 1, 2, 3, 4, BACK).

Once this is perfected, ask the participants to move to a different chair each time you stop. Avoid competition by ensuring there are enough chairs for each participant.

Have a discussion exploring change. What was it like shifting position? Would it have been as rewarding if we had stayed in one place? Did you notice things sounded or looked different each time you moved? How might changing some of the things in your life or workplace influence how you see the world and those around you? What about when we are in conflict with someone – how important might perspective be then?

Note: Adapt this exercise and the subsequent questioning for people with physical disability by not moving but instead swapping between different drums and percussion instruments in the gap of silence – have helpers available to help swap between drums and percussion.

12.6.7 Motivation

IND, GRP, FAM, COR. Age Range: 6 years and up.

Key Focus Areas: Regulation, teamwork, social awareness, communication, self-awareness, persistence.

(A) ARE YOU READY?

Say: 'In this exercise we can each enter the rhythm at our own choosing. We choose what we will play and the time we decide to join those already playing, if we join at all, and we will examine what things influence that timing. Remember – you choose! You don't have to play at all if you don't want to.'

Start a rhythm from the rhythm catalogue (Chapter 10) at a relatively fast tempo, adding an additional challenge to joining in with the rhythm.

Repeat this exercise if people were intimidated by the speed of the rhythm, and this time begin with a slower rhythm.

Discuss differences in motivation between people and between different circumstances – for example, the two different tempos. What sorts of things motivate you generally? What about motivating you out of your comfort zone – what might do that? How important is success to motivation? What about the support you get from others – can that help motivate you? What doesn't work? How might you use this knowledge to help motivate someone else who needed to shift their personal situation?

(B) STOP OR GO

In the middle of the circle, one person (the spotter) should stand at one end facing away from the centre and another one, two or three individuals should stand at the other end. Place a small percussion instrument immediately behind the spotter.

The idea is for the two (or three) individuals to sneak up on the person who is facing away from them without being spotted moving – if the person turns and catches them moving, they return to their chair. If they turn and are stationary, the spotter turns back again.

The remaining drummers should play their Bass notes each time one of the people sneaking up moves. The aim is to grab the percussion instrument without being spotted.

If they succeed, they take it back to their chair and can use it in the next exercise.

What motivated you to play this game? How do these things relate to motivations in other areas of your life? What stopped your progress? What types of things reduce your motivation to move forward in your life? How can teamwork influence motivation?

Note: This will not be suitable for some people with a physical disability.

(C) HANG ON IN THERE

Use the 'Hang On in There' 12.4.3(a) exercise.

Examine the connection between motivation, patience and persistence.

(D) COSTS AND REWARDS

This exercise examines the intrinsic social rewards of belonging, acceptance and recognition and the social cost of exclusion. It can be done as an individual or group exercise.

Divide the group in two – one half should retain their instruments and the other half should not. The half chosen to give up their instruments should place them in the middle of the circle and return to their seats. Tell them that the choice to resume the rhythm, when they are invited to do so, is their choice alone – there's no right or wrong.

Have those still with instruments play a simple, steady beat. At random the practitioner should invites individuals from this half (no instruments) to 'come on in'. On invitation they can choose whether to go and get their instrument or not. Over the course of the exercise each person should receive an invitation to join the group.

Discuss with the members who were originally left out what motivated them to either join in or stay as they were. How do these influences impact your decisions in daily life? Is it sometimes easier to sit life out? What are the dangers of doing too much of that? How important is an invitation to motivate you? What underlies self-motivation?

Swap roles between the two halves and repeat if time allows. In one-to-one work the practitioner should invite the individual they are working with to enter at their leisure and stop whenever they wish, and provide them with a small range of different instruments.

Note: This may not be suitable for people with a physical disability.

(E) SHOULD I STAY OR SHOULD I GO

Players should pair up with another individual sitting directly opposite them in the circle. The aim of the game is to swap seats with your partner in the silence between the rhythm. Each person has to choose when to go, but if one person moves to swap places and the other stays in their chair, then both are out. The pairs should move in order, not all together, with the practitioner determining which pair will move next.

The whole group should start off playing a simple, steady rhythm of their choice and practise stopping and starting the rhythm with a seven-count rest in between (i.e. stopping on the first note of a four-count bar and coming back on the first note of the second bar following that – STOP, 2, 3, 4, 1, 2, 3, 4, BACK). Practise this several times.

Before beginning, emphasise there is freedom of choice – the participants do not have to move.

Explain that if they do move, they need to be seated before the rhythm resumes. If one person in a pair moves and not the other, both are out.

Start the rhythm slowly so people have plenty of time to swap chairs and gradually speed up so that it gets tougher and tougher to make it across.

Extension: In each pair you can have one playing a drum and one playing a percussion instrument – clave, bell or shaker.

Discuss how this game relates to what influences our decision-making processes in general and how other people can impact our decisions, choices and actions for better or worse. Was your decision yours alone? How many of your decisions impact other people? How often do other people's choices impact our lives? Explore the importance of recognising the interconnectivity of people in all dimensions – family, community, nationally, globally.

Note: This may not be suitable for people with a physical disability.

12.6.8 Belonging

IND, GRP, FAM, COR. Age Range: 6 years and up.

Key Focus Areas: Healthy relationships, values, social awareness, creativity, problem solving, communication.

(A) HARMONY

The group should be given a verbal description of harmony and then told that the challenge of this exercise is to each play their own thing but still harmonise with each other.

They must start all together, heads down, playing their own thing (it will sound wild and disconnected) and then they raise their heads and modify their rhythms to connect with each other in harmony – using the same volume and same tempo and leaving space for each to be heard.

Before starting, you may decide to warn the group not to try to 'force people into your rhythm'. If you decide not to warn them, this can often happen and serves as an interesting discussion point in relation to this theme.

Explore the steps the participants took to find a harmonious connection in relation to the steps people might need to take to connect with others.

(B) TRUST ME

Use the 'Trust Me' 12.4.2(a) exercise.

Examine the connection between trust and belonging.

(C) FIND YOUR BASS – FIND YOUR PLACE

Use the 'Find Your Bass – Find Your Place' 12.5.7(a) exercise.

Re-examine the different factors represented by the Bass that serve to connect people in healthy ways.

(D) LAYER IN YOUR RHYTHM

Use the 'Layer In Your Rhythm' 12.5.7(d) exercise.

Explore the skills of social connection and social harmony.

12.6.9 Partnership

IND, GRP, FAM, COR. Age Range: 8 years and up.

Key Focus Areas: Teamwork, communication, creativity, problem solving, values.

(A) GUIDE ME HOME

Issues Addressed: Teamwork, communication, partnership, trust, sound localisation.

Specialist Population: Sensory perception disorders.

Pair people up (sitting next to each other) and ask them to come up with one sound on their instrument that they can identify as a way of recognising each other. Then have one member of each pair enter the middle of the circle and ask them to shut their eyes (or hand out blindfolds). Mix up the people in the middle to disorientate them and then ask their partners to try to help them return to their chair using their special sound code.

   Note: Sometimes it is necessary to only put a small number of people in the middle, as in larger groups the sound can make it impossible to discern specific signals.

Exploring partnerships as a way of meeting life's challenges. What sorts of existing partnerships do you have to help you negotiate life? What are some of the skills you employ to make there relationships work for you? What are some of the obligations partners have to each other? What are some of the things that undermine a partnership? How does balance impact partnership?

(B) ADD YOUR RHYTHM
Use the 'Add Your Rhythm' 12.3.5(a) exercise.

Explore partnership skills and the compromises necessary to work together.

(C) LAYER IN YOUR RHYTHM
Use the 'Layer In Your Rhythm' 12.5.7(d) exercise.

(D) ONE TO THE RIGHT, ONE TO THE LEFT
Use the 'One to the right, One to the left' 12.4.5(a) exercise.

(E) THE TWO-WAY SHUFFLE
Use the 'The Two-Way Shuffle' 16.3(a) exercise.

12.6.10 Vision

IND, GRP, FAM, COR. Age Range: 8 years and up.

Key Focus Areas: Self-belief, confidence, problem solving, teamwork, leadership.

(A) I HAVE A DREAM

Discuss the 'I have a dream' speech by Martin Luther King (for an audio recording see: https://ia600402.us.archive.org/29/items/MLKDream/MLKDream_64kb.mp3).

Ask each person to come up with one statement of a future they would like to see for themselves or their community and write these on a white-board: 'I have a dream that…'

Play a very soft (low volume), simple 4/4 rhythm and upon a signal add the Bass rhythm accent B - B b B (I have a dream). Practise this a few times until it is fluid. Then tell your participants that each time the Bass phrase is played there will be a period of silence where they are asked to close their eyes and visualise their dream coming true.

$$1 + 2 + 3 + 4 +$$

$$B \quad - \quad B b B$$

Then start the rhythm and at the conclusion of each accent ask people to close their eyes and visualise their dream coming true (extend the silent visualisation period for a set number of rests before calling back the rhythm. Repeat.

Discuss the importance of dreams in relation to goals and a better life. Explore the power of visualisation in assisting people with preparing for the steps they may need to take to realise their dreams and meet the challenges of life. Sometimes we see people use visualisation in sport (e.g. imagining the horse clearing the fence). How might you use visualisation to prepare yourself for overcoming a barrier in your life? Can you think of people who have realised their dreams in spite of significant adversity?

(B) SEE IT, THEN PLAY IT

Use the 'See It Then Play It' 12.1.4(e) exercise.

Discuss this exercise with reference to the power of visualisation in problem solving, future planning and creativity.

12.7 Finishing Up – Terminating Counselling or Finishing a Program

At the end of a Rhythm2Recovery course, or a select period of individual therapy, there are a number of points that need to be addressed. First amongst these is to ensure that the finishing process is an open and expected one and that beyond the completion of the work done together, there are in place opportunities for further growth and support – an after-care plan. Additionally, it is important for people to be able to talk about the feelings and thoughts that arise due to the completion of the relationship or to allow this to be expressed musically. The finishing up theme card in the Rhythm2Recovery session card pack focuses on summarising the outcomes of the process to date and empowering the individual or participants to continue their progress into the future.

12.7.1 Exercises for the Final Session
(A) IN A NUTSHELL – PERSONAL TESTIMONIALS

Start the group on a steady pulse and bring the volume right down – invite each person in succession to talk about what they have gained from their time together. The facilitator should start the process by recalling the core themes that have been discussed and then encouraging each person to offer up one thing they have learned or appreciated from the process.

The exercise finishes with the facilitator asking the group members to expand their rhythm to represent the expansion of their understanding and play together in solidarity.

(B) IF IT IS TO BE, THEN IT'S UP TO ME
Use the exercise 'If It Is To Be, Then It's Up To Me' 12.3.8(b)

Emphasise the power of each individual to face the challenges ahead.

(C) FIND YOUR STRENGTHS RHYTHM GAME

Use the 'Find Your Strengths Rhythm Game' 12.5.8(b) exercise.

Reinforce the different strengths individuals take away with them and can use to meet the challenges ahead.

(D) GIVING THANKS

Think about the things in your life that you can be thankful for – it is easy to focus on the things that are going wrong, but it is just as important, if not more so, to focus on the positive things in your life. You can list the positives on a white-board if you like. Get one thing from each person.

Nominate a short rhythm phrase that represents all the positives in your life, and ask people to watch out for that rhythm. Play 'Call and Response' and whenever that rhythm comes up the individual or group must answer it with the pattern Thank-you, Thank-you, Thank-you ve-ry much (B - O - B - O - O o O o O).

1 + 2 + 3 + 4 +	1 + 2 + 3 + 4 +
B O B O	O o O o O

Finish this exercise with the group saying the phrase as they play it.

12.8 Performance

For many people a good way of completing a Rhythm2Recovery program is to organise a short performance (public or private), where they are able to showcase their skills as a team playing music together and where they receive recognition for their effort and progress. It is also a way of giving back to the broader community, as performances often take place in public settings, and it allows for other forms of creativity, including dance and costume design. Successful performances can boost self-esteem, connect people to the world outside of therapy and provide a sense of achievement and mastery that empowers individuals to meet future challenges.

The idea of performing, however, is a very challenging one for many individuals and should never be forced upon people. Not every person or group will be able, or ready, to perform at the conclusion of a program. Performance anxiety is a very prevalent condition but can be mediated by an open and empowering process where the group members decide for themselves where, how and to whom they will perform. My favourite performances are not those where the group perform for an audience, but rather when the group can actively involve the audience as players themselves, whether with spare instruments, clapping, dancing or vocalising. These interactive performances are far less intimidating and break down the walls of separation that many of the individuals in my groups live with on a daily basis. It is vital, prior to deciding upon a course of action, to consider how the purpose of the performance will meet the needs of the individuals you are working with and the types of negative outcomes, anxieties, etc. that are at risk of occurring.

12.9 Ongoing Support

An important consideration for the practitioner at the completion of a Rhythm2Recovery intervention is how progress made during the course of therapy or a psycho-education program can be maintained. It is a disturbing reality that much of the gain made during the period of intervention can be quickly undone if an individual feels a sense of abandonment upon termination, and that for many people who enter therapy this feeling derives from a history of rejection and betrayal and thus is particularly ripe for renewal (Rice and Follette, 2003).

Where a practitioner recognises that the individual or group they are working with has developed an affinity with the rhythmic exercises and drumming of the work, they can suggest a range of options to maintain that connection and the positive outcomes associated with it. High amongst these is to take advantage of the prevalence of recreational drum-circles open to the general public that are to be found in most cities and larger towns around the world. In my own work, one of the ways I handled terminations was to accompany an individual or group to one such community drumming event prior to the end of our work together.

Another option is to support a specific organisation – for example, community mental health service, youth drop-in centre, prison or school – in establishing their own recreational drum-circle. I have seen these flourish as a new place people can come to, with any level of experience, and safely connect to others through community music. They work particularly well when the individuals or students receiving support are given an active role in their organisation. This involvement emphasises their ability to make things happen and influence their own world for the better, and they are further rewarded by providing something of benefit to the broader community.

12.10 Evaluation

The final session is also usually the time to give out evaluative questionnaires and other statistical scales that can be used to assess progress over the course of an intervention. Often these are based on the same measure given out prior to beginning a course of therapy or psycho-social intervention, with the aim of measuring change between entry (pre) results and those at the completion of a program (post). For examples of useful measures see Chapter 17.

12.11 Certificates of Learning

It can be useful, particularly in group programs, to acknowledge the commitment required, and learning gained, from completing a Rhythm2Recovery program, by presenting participants with a certificate of learning such as the one available as download with this book. I have had clients whom I have visited many years later proudly show off their certificate to me, which they hold as a valuable reminder of an important period of their life.

13

RHYTHMIC MOVEMENT

Well before I started using music to enhance my therapeutic practice, I was actively benefiting from using rhythmic movement. I began martial arts training in my early twenties and have continue to exercise in this way. I have been witness to how these, and other forms of rhythmic exercise, improve coordination and build physical confidence and self-esteem in people of all ages and from all walks of life. Like many martial artists, I later extended my passion for rhythmic movement into dance and have watched the power of dance help people improve their physical balance, coordination, cognitive functioning and social integration.

Our increased understanding of the way music impacts the brain has additional implications for individuals who have difficulties with motor control and general physical coordination. Research has shown that rhythmic music impacts areas of the brain associated with movement – the pre-motor cortex, supplementary motor areas, pre-supplementary motor area and the lateral cerebellum – and that a level of synchronisation occurs that can be beneficial in the rehabilitation of movement disorders (Thaut *et al.*, 1999). This synchronisation is based on an entrainment of auditory and motor impulses and not only assists individuals with their timing, but also impacts whole patterns of movement, readily improving motor stability (Kenyon and Thaut, 2000). In my experience, many individuals, particularly those with sensory perception difficulties, who struggle with motor coordination, can benefit from rhythmic movement exercises entrained to a musical pulse.

In the Rhythm2Recovery model we have introduced a number of simple body movement exercises that are aligned to the rhythmic pulse of the music and may assist participants with improved motor control and stability. Music and dance go hand in hand, and in fact in many languages the one word means the same thing. However, for some people the idea of dance is confronting; 'I can't dance' or 'I'm not going to dance in front of you / them' were common remarks heard in my sessions before I moved away from the word 'dance' and replaced it with 'movement'. Few people have a problem with the idea of movement, and when we combine that with repetition and connect the two in time with a musical pulse, it quickly becomes dance. The other way we can help support reticent individuals utilise this element in their therapy is to ensure these exercises are performed together with the practitioner, or with the group as a whole, and not as an individual performance, vulnerable to judgmental observation and heightened self-consciousness.

Coordinated movement can also incorporate the technique of mirroring, where one person imitates another – a technique used to increase empathy, emotional understanding and social bonding between a practitioner and the individual they are supporting or between members of a group (McGarry and Russo, 2011). The motor processes (movement) of one person observed by another stimulates emotional responses that allow us to interpret body language, a critical social skill that is often missing in individuals with sensory perception issues. Mirroring in movement increases mirror neuron activity and can enhance our emotional sensitivity and communication skills.

The range of exercises outlined in this manual are designed to be simple and fun – they are generally not introduced on their own but often surreptitiously as part of a game in order to maximise engagement and minimise shame or self-consciousness.

Exercises include:

- mirroring exercises:

  » 'Move With Me' 12.5.1(a)

  » 'Up and Down' 12.3.5(c)

  » 'Bounce Back (Back on Track)' 12.2.10(a)

  » 'Grow' 12.3.9(a)

- balancing exercises:

  » 'Balance Me' 12.1.4(c)

- stretching and rotating exercises:

  » 'Stretch to the Rhythm' 12.1.4(b)

- cross-directed limb exercises:

  » Tag (You're It!) With Rhythm 12.1.4(d)

  » 'The Two-Way Shuffle' 16.3(a)

- obstacle manoeuvring exercises:

  » 'Friends' 12.3.3(a)

  » 'The Human Maze' 12.6.1(a)

- group coordination exercises:

  » 'Crossing the Line' 12.4.2(c)

  » 'One to the Right, One to the Left' 12.4.5(a)

- improvised expressive exercises:

  » Into the Unknown 12.4.1(b).

13.1 Additional Exercises Utilising Movement

IND and GBP exercises – All ages. May not be suitable for person with physical disabilities.

(A) MINDFUL MOVEMENT
A GROUNDING EXERCISE. SUITABLE FOR BOTH GROUPS AND INDIVIDUALS

Start with all of the group standing (move drums and chairs a short distance away), planting the feet at shoulder width, bending the knees slightly and focusing on pushing into the floor. Say: 'Focus on cementing your body, through your feet, into the floor below, so that you feel grounded, solid, stable, and firmly connected to the earth. Slow your breath, and as you breathe out, push down and strengthen that connection each time. If other thoughts come to mind, recognise them and then come back to this focus on entering your body and connecting to the earth.'

After approximately three minutes ask half the group to return to their seats and regain their drums (every second person in the circle) and every other person to move into the middle of the circle.

The people in the middle should walk in a circular route, in the same direction, in time to a slow Bass pulse played by the other drummers and focus as much as possible on their walk.

Say: 'Start off by standing still and regaining that connection you had before. Now walk slowly, and focus on your walk, how your feet touch the floor. Notice the transference of weight between your feet. Notice the bend in your knees and the movement of your hips. If other thoughts come to mind, acknowledge them and bring your focus back to your feet. Notice any sensations from their connection to the ground each time you step. Notice the different pressure of each part of the foot's connection.'

After approximately three minutes stop the group in the middle and finish with a short focus on grounding before reversing parts – the drummers should move to the middle while the walkers go back to drumming. Repeat the exercise.

(B) MOVE TO THE MIDDLE

Allocate members of the group to two teams using alternate seats. Every time there is a break in the rhythm one team (alternate teams) must enter the middle and perform a coordinated group movement.

Play a steady rhythm as a group and count down from four to STOP – hold the silence for seven counts then re-enter the rhythm (i.e. stop on the first note of a four-count bar and come back on the first note of the second bar following that: STOP, 2, 3, 4, 1, 2, 3, 4, START).

In the silence, people should move quickly to the middle and perform different movements – ask your group to come up with ideas. High fives are good options, as are leg rises with linking arms

Do different body moves in the gap and return by the eighth count to resume playing.

Extension: Play tonal chimes (pentatonic scale) or other percussion in the gap.

(C) FREEZE

Teach the rhythm break sequence where we stop the rhythm on a signal for a set number of beats and then resume playing. In the break participants have to freeze their body movement and facial expression until the resuming count. Silly faces are good!

Extension: Ask every second person in the group to enter the middle of the circle and focus on their walking. Have them move randomly to the music but on a specific sound (e.g. a bell), their group must freeze. Any found unbalanced at this point must return to their seat.

(D) COUNT AND MOVE

One chair is chosen as the 'director's chair' and the person sitting in that chair decides how many places the group will move (moving in one direction) by playing a number between one and four on the bell each time the facilitator halts the rhythm (this is the only bell in the room).

Play a simple 4/4 rhythm and immediately after the facilitator counts down to STOP (for a count of eight), the person in the director's chair should play their bell. The number of strikes they play will determine how many seats in a clockwise direction the group members move, before they resume their rhythm.

(E) STATUES

Half the participants should enter the middle of the circle and spread out so they are not touching – then they should be asked to pose like a statue and not move.

On a signal from the facilitator the drummers should play a single note Bass pulse and the people in the middle can move one step for each note – not touching anyone else.

As soon as the pulse stops, they must freeze as a statue again. Touching anyone or moving in the silence takes you back to your chair. Vary the Bass tempo to make it more challenging.

13.2 Body Percussion

Body percussion is another wonderful way of introducing people to rhythmic music without the need for props of any kind. It combines the benefits of music and movement and most importantly develops an increased awareness of the body. We know that for many people who have experienced trauma, and for the many individuals with sensory perception disorders, a disassociation with the body is present that amplifies their condition and reduces opportunities for social integration and recovery (Emmons and McKendry Anderson, 2005; Ogden, 2006; Van Der Kolk, 2014). Body percussion that emphasises grounding techniques by connecting the feet to the floor is particularly helpful in supporting those who feel a weightlessness that leaves them disconnected from, and unbalanced in their physical selves.

The basic building blocks of body percussion include:

- C: Clapping – different hand combinations and hand shapes (open fingers, closed fingers)

- CL: Clicking – fingers and thumbs

- T: Tapping – different body areas including chest, shoulders, stomach, sides, thighs and buttocks

- S: Stomping – of the legs and feet

- R: Rubbing – of the hands

- TH: Thumping – body beat using the thumb end of a clenched fist on the chest or into the palm of the opposite hand.

I like to start these sequences with people sitting and do some simple 'Call and Response' exercises (see Section 12.1.1) or 'Simon Says' to build confidence. For more complex patterns, each of the body percussion elements can be put into rhythmic sequences that will harmonise with each other by allocating one movement to a specific count in the bar. So to start a simple body percussion rhythm song, have your participants stand in the circle. Ask everyone to vocalise a simple four-count backing beat (1, 2, 3, 4, repeat). When this is steady, attach one movement to each beat or try out the patterns below.

Basic Body Percussion Drills

Timing	1 + 2 + 3 + 4 +	1 + 2 + 3 + 4 +	1 + 2 + 3 + 4 +	1 + 2 + 3 + 4 +
Part 1	C C T T	C C CL -	C C T T	C C CL -
Part 2	S S C C	S S TH -	S S C C	S S TH -
Part 3	T T TH -	T T CL CL	T T TH -	T T CL CL
Part 4	R R R R	T T T T	R R R R	T T T T

For further body percussion arrangements, each of the rhythms in the drumming catalogue (Chapter 10) can be transcribed to body percussion, enabling you to do different rhythm harmonies by allocating different members different patterns, and there are many more examples available online.

14

RHYTHMIC VOICE

The use of the rhythmic voice in the Rhythm2Recovery program is a limited one due to the fearful and anxiety-provoking relationship some individuals have with singing, particularly in front of others. The paramount focus on safety within the Rhythm2Recovery model reduces the scale of what is well recognised as another powerful medium for emotional expression, identity formation and communication (Austin, 2008). Introducing individuals to finding their voice in a non-threatening way, means:

- avoiding a focus on correct tone, pitch or timing

- replacing words with sounds

- providing plenty of encouragement

- ensuring there is no element of competitiveness present

- ensuring the process is fun, rather than too serious or introspective.

Singing or chanting is common in healing traditions around the world and can act on a number of fronts to improve recovery. Singing impacts the breath and can help individuals whose breath is shallow or anxious, by encouraging deeper breathing and, by association, lowering heart rate, calming the stress response and improving the level of homeostasis. Singing also helps people reconnect to their physical selves and allows them to give expression to thoughts and feelings that might otherwise be repressed (Austin, 2001). Singing in groups offers a range of benefits associated with the rewards of social interaction, connection and belonging (Clift *et al.*, 2008).

Chanting – rhythmic vocalisation – has been used in many different cultural traditions, for spiritual, healing and academic purposes. Chanting has been shown to slow respiration and induce calm, as well as improve concentration and memory (Bernardi et al., 2001). The mental clarity and calmness induced by soft, repetitive chanting can be additionally reinforced when synchronised with soft, repetitive musical rhythms. Chanting is commonly used to reinforce the memory and recall of important facts and details and thus can help embed important learning concepts in social and emotional understanding. In the Rhythm2Recovery model, verbal chants are developed by individuals to reflect upon identity and social and emotional awareness and to reinforce affirmations, as well as to assist with internalising attitudes and behaviour.

14.1 Rhythmic Vocal Exercises

IND and GRP. Age Range: 8 years and up.

(A) BREATH TO SOUND
MARY KNYSH, DAVID DARLING

One of the easiest ways to start people singing was taught to me by Mary Knysh and starts by utilising the breath. Start by doing some focused breathing exercises – in through the nose and out through the mouth; you may also find an upward arm movement on the in-breath and a downward arm movement on the out-breath helps to accent each action and improve focus. Once this is occurring at a relaxed and even pace, ask people to breathe out one note (vocal tone) of their choice on their next out-breath and hold it (the facilitator should conduct this release by moving their hand away from their mouth in a flowing gesture and performing a stop cut to finish the note). Try this several times together on the out-breath.

The group should release this note together, reducing self-consciousness and shame. It is also important to remind people that there are no wrong notes – this is not a competitive exercise. In larger groups, the facilitator may subdivide participants into smaller teams of three or four and practise releasing these communal notes in smaller groups one after the other. Participants should be asked to try to find a connection between their sound and the sound of others in the same group and to adjust their note if necessary.

Have the group move closer together and take them through some further rounds, this time changing the volume to louder and softer. Finish by having the group bring their volume down slowly so that it fades away to nothing.

Once this exercise has been tried a number of times, participants' confidence in their voice increases and these sounds and harmonies can be incorporated into the drum-circle or transformed gradually into songs with words.

(B) CALL AND RESPONSE

When you do 'Call and Response' on the drum it is easy to add some vocal chants – always start with something humorous and make sure you use your hands to show that you are expecting a response (open hands, palms up and directed outwards towards the group). Sometimes I start with animal noises or nonsensical phrases like 'Do Wa, Do Wa' and 'Shoobee, Doobee, Do' and these can then be extended into scat phrases like 'Boobalee, Do, Baaa, Ba, Do, Ba, Do', which usually end up being ridiculously long and leave people collapsed with laughter as they respond.

Other phrases such as 'Whose got the Rhythm?' – 'I've got the Rhythm!' or 'Can you feel that Beat?' – 'I can feel that Beat' help to encourage and focus the group on the rhythmic timing of the music and in particular the pulse. Rather than do pure vocal 'Call and Response', I find that when it is interspersed with instrumental 'Call and Response' it is less intimidating and the two complement and reinforce each other – the voice becoming just another fun instrument to play.

(C) THE FOOTBALL CHANT

GRP.

Many people have heard the chanting football crowds do in support of their teams. This is a non-intimidating and culturally acceptable way for boys, in particular, to find and use their singing voice. If you have people with a history of cheerleading in your group, you can make them group leaders.

Divide and separate the group into two teams and ask them to come up with a team name and then a team chant each (acceptable language required). Give some examples of what a team chant might sound like:

- 'We are the Titans, We are the Titans, Strong , Brave, Not Frightened, Strong, Brave, Not Frightened.'

- 'Rivals, Rivals, You Should Fear, The Midland Boys Are Here.'

- 'Watch Out One, Watch Out All, You're Up Against Us and You're Going To Fall' etc.

Go around the different groups and help out if they get stuck – ensure they practise their chant as a team.

Bring the groups back together and start a simple, slow and steady pulse (one person from each team may play a Bass drum). Ask them to visualise being on either side of a football pitch (use another sport if this is not relevant). Then ask one team to start and the other to answer, telling them that passion for their team is what you are most looking for.

Finally, once the chants are established and answering each other, play with different dynamics – slowing it right down, speeding it up and finally fading away.

Once the practice of chanting is established, it can be utilised to accentuate learning in other areas, with participants devising short chants that represent their awareness and understanding of concepts drawn from the themes of different sessions. These include:

- Values – 'Tolerance, Loyalty, Respect and Truth – These Are My Values, These Are My Roots'.

- Boundaries – 'Hold the Line, What's Mine Is Mine, Hands off Brother and We'll Be Fine'.

- Strengths – 'Bravery, Honesty and Generosity: Three of My Personal Qualities'.

- Identity – 'I Observe Myself, I Respect Myself, I Know Myself and I Grow Myself'.

- Self-belief – 'If It's Going to Be, Then It's up to Me'.

- Emotional intelligence – 'Let Go of Anger, Let Go of Blame, Let Go of the Past and Live Again'.

- Affirmations – 'I'm Going to Make the Most of Life, Nurture My Friendships and Do What's Right'.

(D) THE VOCAL YAWN
ADAPTED FROM B.MCAFEE

This is a good exercise if you have an individual or people in your group who are tired or unresponsive and you want to liven them up and have a laugh.

You can implement it purposefully, but I often do it when I notice someone yawning, by saying: 'Hey, can I borrow your yawn for a minute?' Ask people to take a good long yawn and then vocalise the outward breath part of it. This practice can help reduce tension in the throat or jaw that often impacts a singing voice.

Facilitate a song of yawns by first identifying different pitches of people's yawns and then having them come in over the top of each other in sequence. Finish with very soft yawning, people going to sleep and snoring.

A fun way to change it is to add a 'yawning break' into a rhythm-circle – start a rhythm with your group and count down to a break (4, 3, 2, 1, STOP) before having people yawn together or in a prearranged sequence for a set count before resuming the rhythm.

(E) RAP IT
SEE 'FIND YOUR VOICE' 12.6.5(A)

Rap music, the musical expression of the hip hop culture, is a powerful and transformative musical genre of central importance to many young people in cultures around the world. Using the musical vernacular of the individuals we work with within our work is central to a culturally sensitive approach. Rap music embodies a social force that articulates many of the concerns and issues confronting young people in today's society. Rap relies on simple syncopated rhythms for its basis and the hand-drum can replicate these rhythms to a degree. Scratching the skin of the hand-drum with the fingernails can also be used to replicate the turntable technique of moving a vinyl record back and forth whilst manipulating the crossfader of a DJ mixer. The music, and specifically the intention of the lyrics in 'rap', are magnified by the repetition of its rhythmic pulse.

In the Rhythm2Recovery model we encourage small groups to work together to find 'rhymes' that fit into a standard 4/4 rhythm, across a 16-note (4 x 4) or four-bar measure. It can be useful to have one person (a co-facilitator) maintain a steady pulse on the first note of each bar to assist individuals with their timing. The lyrics themselves should be aligned to the theme of a session and, like the chanting exercise 'The Football Chant' 14.1(c), can be readily adapted to a wide range of subject areas whilst illuminating a personal perspective. Once the lyrics are completed, the group can move on to adding different music effects to complement them – extra beats, scratches, clapping, beat-boxing and dance moves.

Reflection on the lyrical content (sometimes written on a white-board) after the musical expression itself forms the final stage of these exercises, where individual ideas, thoughts and feelings can be discussed.

(F) A CONVERSATION IN PYGMY

When I was a bit younger (OK, a lot younger!), I travelled through central Africa and spent some time living with the Mbuti pygmies in the Congo. One of the extraordinary things about that experience was their use of language, which was sung rather than spoken. All language for the Mbuti was expressed in a singing voice, which had evolved as an effective way of increasing the range of their communication through the thick jungle that was their home environment.

In this exercise, which requires a reasonable degree of trust and confidence, the individual or participants are asked to sing a conversation. Each person participates in the conversation using singing to voice their questions, statements or responses. A conversation about the joys and trepidations of singing can be a good, humorous topic to start this exercise. Encourage people to experiment with different tones, pitch and volume. The naming games 12.1.3(b), (d) and (e) can also be easily adapted to this exercise; instead of 'See It. Then Play It' 12.1.4(e), you can instead 'Sing It, Then Play It'.

Singing is also a useful way to create a new rhythm – people can be asked to find a short phrase that can be transposed onto the drum. If possible, work in pairs so that one person signs the rhythm while another interprets it on their drum; then once a regular pattern is established, the remaining members can join in.

(G) WAKE UP YOUR FACE
ADAPTED FROM B.MCAFEE

This exercise breathes life into tired facial features. Ask the individual or participants you are working with to make a 'WOW' sound with their voice, while at the same time expressing the surprise associated with that word through their facial features and simultaneously turning towards you or another group member. That member passes the 'WOW' over to another person of their choice in the same way and so the game goes on.

Next, have people stand and extend the 'WOW' sound so that it becomes drawn out like a low hum and have people focus on their diaphragm, placing a hand over this part of their body, just below the navel, and observing the contraction as they inhale and the expansion on the outward breath. Maintain the low hum and extend this focus to the feet and the feeling of being grounded to the floor, and below that, connecting to the earth itself. Ask people to focus on that connection as they continue that low hum and close their eyes if they feel comfortable. Keep the hum going for as long as possible before taking a breath and repeating it. After a while, allow the hum to fade and remain silent for approximately 30 seconds after the last audible note.

He who sings, frightens away his ills.

Cervantes

15

FIVE KEY ANALOGIES

The use of analogies in the Rhythm2Recovery model is central to extending the lessons of the experience to the awareness of the mind. Throughout history people have used analogy and its extended form, metaphor, often in the form of stories or fables, to communicate wisdom, values, morals, standards and appropriate behaviour; using language from one field of experience and applying it to another. The use of analogies and metaphors, above and beyond the use of facts or statistics to impart knowledge and understanding, derives from the safety of using symbols to give meaning to events in our lives – safety through the avoidance of a direct association with an individual's story and instead using images that reduce the confronting nature of overt personal exposure. This safety is also characterised by the freedom of the receiver to draw from the metaphor their own associations and meaning as it relates to their life experience. Analogies and metaphors also help people clarify concepts that otherwise remain beyond their understanding, by shifting perspective, removing blockages and opening doors to growth.

Most of the analogies we use in the Rhythm2Recovery model are simple forms that showcase similarities between the experience in the drum-circle or playing the drum, to a range of relational issues. Participation in the drum-circle itself is a social activity, whilst playing the drum is a form of both physical and emotional communication; hence there exists a wide range of parallels that can be drawn from these experiences to awaken understanding in other relational areas of life. Extending these analogies across different exercises and into ongoing sessions helps embed the connection between the therapeutic experience and real life and any additional awareness it brings forth. Aligning analogies and metaphors to the therapeutic needs of the participants requires an awareness of the presenting issues and a focus on the purpose of the metaphor and how it can be utilised to help achieve a therapeutic goal.

15.1 Finding Your Bass (Base)

This analogy draws on the basic evolutionary need for safety. Within the Rhythm2Recovery model, the Bass note, in the centre of the drum, is seen as a place of safety – a place to return to when lost in the complexity of a rhythm. The Bass note connects directly with the pulse of the rhythm – the same beat we automatically entrain to with our bodies as we tap along or dance to a piece of music. At the beginning of any session, whether educational or therapeutic, reminding people of a place of safety prior to beginning a new experience is comforting.

FIND YOUR BASS – FIND YOUR PLACE
Use the 'Find your Bass – Find your Place' 12.5.7(a) exercise.

For many of the people we work with, life is often unsafe. Many people have experiences of trauma, abandonment, violence and loss. Locating a safe place is one of the keys to survival in the face of such adversity and uncertainty. For many substance users, using their drug of choice takes them to that safe place, whilst for others, safety is defined by the four walls of their bedroom or the company of a close friend. By using the Bass note to represent the concept of a base or foundation of safety, we can explore with participants the importance of having such a place in their lives, what contributes to their sense of safety, how to extend that sense of safety into other areas of their lives and how to support others they care about (including their children) by providing them with a similar, stable foundation.

This concept of base or foundation links closely to the importance given to value formation in the Rhythm2Recovery format, which is also a key part of the ACT model. Clarity of values provides us with a foundation for life. Knowing what is important to an individual helps provide a direction and purpose that many people find missing from their lives, as well as profoundly influencing behaviour.

15.2 A Life of Rhythm

This analogy utilises the primal place of rhythm in our lives, how these rhythms impact us and our relationships and how they change over the course of our lives. Rhythm can reflect any personal, reoccurring behaviour, such as playing computer games, smoking ganja, gambling or riding your bike to work.

The applications are endless, as almost all human behaviour falls into patterns or cycles. The individual, in conjunction with their practitioner, can explore the impact of a pattern of behaviour on their health, their relationships, their career and their happiness, and how it fits with their values and the rhythms (patterns) of other people and the environment.

The rhythm analogy examines parallels between rhythm in music to rhythm in life. One of the key points discussed is the impact of the pace of rhythm and how, as we pick up speed, it gets harder to hold the rhythm stable. In modern life, the pace of life, accentuated by technology, has been linked to a wide range of stressors and health complaints (Read, 2006). Rhythm is often perceived in terms of stability – as stable rhythms and unpredictable rhythms. When the rhythms of our life are stable, such as our sleeping patterns, our diet, our friendships, etc., we generally feel more comfortable and secure – rhythms offer us a sense of security because of their predictable nature. When these rhythms become unstable, such as when our sleeping pattern is regularly disturbed, we eat irregularly or when our relationships become tumultuous, we 'get thrown' and life becomes uncomfortable and insecure.

The security aspect of patterned behaviour can also work against us by impacting our motivation to change when the pattern, though comfortable and reassuring, is doing us harm. This is clear in working with addictive behaviours where people often feel much more comfortable maintaining the same problematic patterns than changing to something new and healthy that remains unknown and thus engenders fear. The same metaphor also extends to the negative impact of peers and family members who may be exercising influence that is working against the future happiness of the individual but represents their only relational bond, providing a sense of security and belonging. In Rhythm2Recovery the practitioner can explore these types of issues through activities that showcase the challenges of breaking free from an unhelpful rhythm.

The analogy of rhythm can also be used to look at the internal patterns that impact our physiology, such as our heartbeat, which provides us with a rhythmic indicator of our physical state, and also our cognitive patterns or thought processes and how elements of these, such as obsessive or compulsive thoughts, can impact our psychology. On a grander scale, rhythms can be used to provide insight into the natural patterns of the earth upon which we live and how these are changing (some in response to global warming) and impacting our lives.

For individuals who have suffered at the hands of natural disasters, such as floods, fires or earthquakes, these discussions often focus on the feeling of powerlessness we have when the rhythm of life suddenly shifts and the challenges of adjusting our rhythm in response.

(See Section 1.2 for further examples of the use of this analogy.)

15.3 The Drum as Your Voice, The Drum as Your Heart

Drumming is a medium of communication, described by many as a 'language of emotion' that can 'reach beyond the power of words'. Throughout history, drums have been used to relay messages and to communicate orders or announcements. In fact, there is a specific drum in Africa (called the 'Talking Drum') that imitates the tonal qualities of the voice. In other cultures, drums were used by the governing hierarchies to communicate with their communities (Chatto, 1996).

This element of drumming allows us to follow the analogy of drumming as it relates to inter-personal communication in its many dimensions. For many of the individuals we work with, communication issues lie at the heart of their relational problems. Given the central importance of communication in relationships generally, this metaphor has significant importance as an educational tool in a range of settings, including corporate development, as well as in therapeutic practice. In the Rhythm2Recovery model we examine the key communication skills of listening and responding through the different 'Call and Response' routines, and have a number of targeted exercises for those with communication deficits, including sound localisation issues.

Efficient communication using the drum relies on a number of factors, which each have relevance for communication generally. These include the clarity of the message itself as it is relayed and the level of attention it receives from the recipient. Details that impact these two core aspects of the communication cycle can be seen in musical language and how readily it is interpreted correctly and responded to, or not. The complexity of a message has a clear correlation to how well it is understood, as does the timing of when it was sent. Correct timing helps align the musicians as they play together and poor timing does just the opposite – how much communication fails due to poor timing?

The way people communicate generally can also be examined in concrete terms by having individuals communicate with each other in the session using their drums. These conversations can then be analysed for clues about what types of issues might be impacting their communication in real life, and the same exercise can be replayed on a regular basis to build skills in this area. These exercises have been particularly useful in my work with children with autism, whose communication skills are an ongoing barrier to social inclusion, and between family members who have become estranged. As a reflection of community diversity, it is common to find both dominant and submissive drummers in the drum-circle and easy to utilise this to explore the impact of power dynamics on communication. We might also examine the phrase 'The best drummers play the fewest notes' in relation to dominating communicators or leadership generally. Each of these exercises provides a safe, and often fun, vehicle for what might otherwise be a confronting look at a particularly personal issue.

The drum is also an important tool for the expression of emotion and, as mentioned previously, we often talk about the drum as a safe 'vessel in which to pour your feelings'. Drums are used to express a wide range of emotions in music and can thus be used to assist individuals to express, release and identify feelings for themselves. In my work I have met many individuals who struggle to name or identify their feelings – the term 'Alexithymia' is given to this condition. For these individuals, the use of the age-old therapeutic mantra 'How did that feel?' is either met with a blank stare or with more overt resistance. Often, however, these same people are more than willing to 'Play how that felt' and this physical activity seems to act as a lubricant in assisting them to recognise and name those feelings that had earlier eluded them.

Playing with feeling on the drum is a critical part of making good rhythmic music and allows us to explore the positive aspects of emotion and how it enhances our relationships. We look at a wide range of other issues connected to our emotions and how they impact us, our perceptions, our behaviours and those around us. Some of the different issues open to this metaphor include the way we are impacted by each other's emotions and the dominance of powerful feelings like anger and resentment. We can explore the repercussions of holding feelings inside and constructive ways for their release (of which one is music), and we can also look closely at exercises that allow us to take control of our feelings, and maintain our equilibrium as oppsed to relinquishing ourselves to their control (see Chapter 11).

15.4 Team Harmony

Playing music with other people usually means working together towards creating a harmonious sound. This simple fact means that delivery of the Rhythm2Recovery model allows us to examine a wide range of elements that impact people's ability to work together. For many people who enter counselling or who are referred to social and emotional learning programs in schools, working well with others is challenging. Their social skills are often low, as is their emotional intelligence. These deficits are often combined with histories of dysfunction within the family and insecure attachment. This inability to collaborate also impacts families when spouses are in conflict and unable to negotiate, as well as larger organisations whose employees are at cross-purposes. Teams generally can't function when team members are at each other's throats, and many business organisations suffer from a toxic work environment due to staff members who are unable to work well with others.

When we are in harmony together as drummers or musicians, we are exercising a number of skills; and equally, when we struggle to find a harmonious connection, we are abdicating those same elements. The practitioner can use this analogy to prompt the individual or group to reflect on these areas and how they can be utilised to improve the way they work with, or relate to, others in a range of different contexts. Harmony in the drum-circle, unlike other musical forms that rely on specific relationships of instrumental pitch, is created through tonal and rhythmic alignment and balance. These two concepts of 'alignment' and 'balance' are central to healthy and harmonious personal relationships and are sometimes referred to as 'rapport'.

We often have a sense of when parts of our lives, including our personal relationships, are out of balance, just as we recognise losing our physical balance. We can explore balance in a wide range of life and social contexts. In our drum play with an individual, or in the drum-circle with a larger group of people, balance is often compromised by different volumes, different tempos or a failure to connect two rhythms to a core pulse. In our relationships we can use these markers to examine how communication between people is impacted by differences in power or assertiveness (volume), by conflicts in the pace of the daily rhythms of our lives (tempo) or by a lack of synergy or common ground (core pulse). The earlier concept of the pulse being marked by the Bass note, which represents a stable foundation, allows us to extend this metaphor into examining differences in values and other core beliefs that affect cooperation.

15.5 Community Drum

In group practice the drum-circle represents a community, working together, playing together, sharing with each other, supporting each other, disagreeing with each other, annoying each other, tolerating each other, working things out together, etc. For many of the individuals I work with in the drum-circle, and for more and more people generally, a connection to community with its sense of belonging and acceptance is hard to find. Loneliness is becoming endemic in our individualised culture and is the major cause of depression – our biggest mental health concern (Eckersly, 2006).

Music helps facilitate social connection for people to whom it does not come easily. The Rhythm2Recovery model allows the practitioner to draw parallels between this musical experience and the challenges of community connection generally. Multiple exercises in the Rhythm2Recovery format involve individuals aligning their rhythms to those of a larger group, with one of the major barriers to connection being the fear of change – for example, 'This rhythm has worked for me in the past, so I'm sticking to it.' The changing rhythms of the drum-circle imitate the changing nature of community and the different social norms present in different communities. Participants learn to adapt their rhythm to changing circumstances, freeing themselves from unproductive rhythms (patterns/habits) that have increased their isolation in the past.

The musical output of the drum-circle reflects the make up, skills and commitment of its members, just as the production of a community of any type does. Today many of us live in a multicultural society where the mix of different people from different backgrounds adds to the richness of our experience as members of these diverse communities. Tolerance, and an appreciation of difference, are issues that can be explored using these types of musical metaphors. I have worked closely with communities where there has been inter-racial conflict using this process and seen first hand its potential to break down divisions. Similarly, this analogy can be extended to explore the many challenges that come from this same level of diversity – how do you combine drums with bells and bells with shakers, etc? This has been a useful analogy for our work with refugees who are experiencing the many difficulties of assimilation.

15.6 Extending Analogy to Metaphor

Given the focus on safety for people resistant to talk-based therapies within this model, most of the analogies used in conjunction with Rhythm2Recovery exercises are brief in nature. However, longer, therapeutic metaphors or stories can be used to help people clarify a concept pertaining to their presenting issues. Storytelling, in the right hands, can quickly build a bond between the storyteller (practitioner) and the individuals or participants they are working with. Storytelling assists people to see new perspectives and helps them access their thoughts and feelings, as well as develop a deeper understanding of the issue before them (Blenkiron, 2011). Of all the many interventions I have seen imposed on indigenous cultures dealing with the aftermath of colonisation – traditional storytelling that accentuated values, boundaries and cultural identity was amongst the most transformational.

One way to extend the rhythmic metaphor in order to help an individual reappraise an issue that comes up for them in therapy is to find an individual, animal or object whose rhythm journey can be used to replicate the individual's own journey or replicate an alternative, but foreseeable, journey. Often I encourage individuals or participants to play both the rhythms and emotions of the story character between different phases of the tale. Some of the key characters that I have used include the following.

The Gardener

The gardener was famous for his vegetables, which won prizes at the local show. Each season the gardener followed the same rhythm of tilling his vegetable beds, fertilising with manure and sowing his crops. In spring he planted tomatoes and corn; in summer he planted melons and turnips; in autumn in went his potatoes; and in winter he planted greens. He'd always worked with this rhythm in the garden, year in and year out, and his dedication had rewarded him with large crops that made his neighbours envious. Things started to get difficult for the gardener when the climate started to change; there was less rain, the summers were getting longer and the days hotter. His routine stayed the same, but his crop was suffering. One year all the melons shrivelled for lack of water and the tomatoes and corn fell off their stalks before ripening. The gardener had always worked the same way as his father had done, and he was sure things would get back to normal – he wasn't going to alter a routine (rhythm) that had done him proud year after year. But things didn't go back the way they were, and eventually the gardener had to face the fact that he would have to change if he was going to grow decent crops again, and that's just what he did! He planted earlier in the season, watered a touch more in summer, installed some shade cloth over his tomatoes and corn to protect them from the sun, and soon enough he was back growing prize-winning vegetables.

The Woman Warrior

In ancient China, all the grand masters of the martial arts were strong, proud, and sometimes arrogant, men. At the time of this story, the Chinese people were ruled by cruel leaders called the Manchus, and there was much discontent. The leaders of the Shaolin temple summoned all the best fighters together to design a fighting system that could be taught quickly to defeat the cruel rulers. Among those who came was a young Buddhist nun, Ng Mui (pronounced Nung Mee). Ng Mui was laughed at by the others for being a woman, small and weak, but she let those taunts float past her. She knew something that the others didn't – that force and power were not necessary to succeed and could easily be turned against an enemy. Ng Mui had watched a fight between a crane and a fox and saw how easily the crane deflected the fox's attack. When the time came for the masters to show their fighting style it was Ng Mui who prevailed. Instead of meeting force with force, she turned the force set against her back onto her attackers and defeated them with their own energy. Ng Mui is credited with inventing the martial art 'Wing Chun', the same fighting style Bruce Lee learned as a boy.

The Train

The train is stuck to the track. This story explores the limitations and frustrations of the train that cannot leave the track and keeps repeating the same circuit, day in and day out, until one day a linesman shifts the points to allow the train onto a new route and a new world of discovery. The train is fearful about entering the new line, but slowly builds up the courage to change its routine and start on down the new track. This new world it enters has its own challenges, as the train must cross bridges it has never been over before, go through tunnels (periods of darkness), climb mountains and stop at new stations, but with all these challenges comes a realisation that the world is full of new possibilities.

The Horse

The horse is controlled by its rider – a mean, strict and dominating individual, who only rides it occasionally, sometimes uses a whip to make it jump or go faster and keeps the horse locked in a small paddock. One day a storm occurs (play the storm) and the frightened horse jumps the yard fence and runs away, galloping as far and fast as its four legs can take it. It gallops on and on, through forests, across swamps, over rivers, scared – running, running, running. Eventually it can run no further and it stops to rest. A young girl sees the frightened horse and gently approaches it. The horse is distrustful of humans, having belonged to a mean owner, but is too tired to run and so permits the girl to take care of it. With time the girl wins the horse's confidence and they ride together exploring new horizons, safe in each other's company.

The Ship

The rhythm of the ship is controlled by the swells of the sea. For years the ship has sailed a safe, stable passage between two ports in protected waters. Then one day, seemingly like any other, its compass fails and its engine stalls. It finds itself lost at sea, buffeted by large waves, rocking to and fro and coming close to being swamped. The captain is scared but remembers his/her training and throws out a sea anchor to provide some stability; the anchor steadies the ship and helps it find its balance. Then the captain radios for assistance and shortly afterwards some tug boats arrive. They cast out ropes to secure the ship and help bring it back to calmer waters and safety.

> *The sound of the drum is the heartbeat of our mother earth. The circle is the symbol of equality.*
>
> *Ojibway proverb*

The Old Car

The old car is feeling neglected. For years it has been running smoothly, but some funny squeaks can be heard under the bonnet and rust has started to appear on the body. The owner of the old car has another newer car that they spend most of their time with, and the old car has been feeling abandoned and unappreciated. One day the owner decides to take the old car for a drive to renew their acquaintance, but halfway up a steep hill the old car stops, broken down, and has to be taken to the service centre. The old car frets that its owner will now reject it; it feels hopeless and worthless compared with its rival, the new car. But after a new service, the old car comes back fitter than ever, climbing the hill is a breeze and its owner welcomes it back home, promising to take better care of it in the future.

The River

The river flows gently between the different towns that line its bank. The river is a source of comfort for many people as well as many animals – the fishermen who feed their families from its waters, the children who swim when it is hot, the gazelles and zebras who drink from it when thirsty. One night there is a big storm (play the storm) and the next day a young girl walks down to the river and decides to go for a swim. She frolics in the shallows for a while and then stretches out and swims towards the middle. Suddenly she finds herself out of her depth and being dragged along by the fast-flowing current – the storm has increased the flow of the river. She struggles against it, trying to swim towards the bank and its shallow water where she can regain her footing, but as she does so she feels herself quickly weakening, going under. Her father sees her in distress and yells to her, 'Don't fight it – go with the current.' Doing just that she focuses on keeping her head up, but not struggling against the strong current, instead allowing it to take her downstream. After a while the river bends and the current comes close to the bank where her father is waiting to catch hold of her and bring her to safety.

16

ADDITIONAL GAMES
AND EXERCISES

16.1 Exercises for Emotional Awareness

IND, GRP, FAM. Age Range: 8 years and up.

(A) NAME THAT EMOTION

Using the drum or facial expressions, or both, one person demonstrates an emotion and the other has to name it.

Examine how easily we can misinterpret feelings and the consequences of doing so.

(B) CONTRASTING EMOTIONS

One person should play their drum with a particular emotion – the person opposite should play the opposite emotion. For example: sad/happy, fearful/ brave, angry/calm, jealous/supportive, etc. Probe for feelings associated with different emotions.

(C) A STORM OF FEELING

Issues Addressed: Emotional awareness, anger management.

Imagine your different feelings and emotions are like a storm building. Play a rain storm with the group. Start off with light rubbing on the drum head, then pitter/patter made with the fingertips, followed gradually by more rapid beats

(Tones) and working your way up to a big Bass rumble, and then reverse the order as the storm fades away.

Who has had feelings build like that? How did you let loose your thunder? What helps people move through their feelings in a productive way?

(D) A BALL OF FEELINGS

Introduce the metaphor of a beach ball representing our feelings and emotions and asking people to support each other by keeping those feelings up – keeping the imaginary beach ball in the air using rumble energy. Say: 'We start as a group lifting the ball as high as we can with our combined energy and then lowering it as low as we can before raising it to a median level, all the time tracking it with our eyes.'

Discuss the challenges of staying positive and the support we can give each other in keeping our spirits up.

Say: 'Then we pass it on to one person's drum and ask them to showcase where their emotions are at present – low or high – before they pass it to another person using their eyes to track the ball as it moves between players, each person expressing the level of their feelings using rumble energy and the height of the imaginary beach ball denoted by the level of their gaze.'

Discuss the changing nature of feelings, the sharing of feelings and the energy required to sustain our feelings – noting how much you have to put out to keep that ball in the air as an individual, compared with when you are getting the support of others.

The exercise also develops teamwork, emotional control and self-awareness. In individual work, I have found this exercise useful in helping clients express how they are feeling and exploring the same concepts but with a more personal focus.

(E) RUMBLE IN THE JUNGLE

Start by recalling the epic boxing match between George Foreman and Muhammad Ali in Zaire in 1974. George Foreman was much bigger and stronger than Ali and expected to win. Ali spent most of the fight avoiding contact, dancing around George, until he was exhausted.

Discuss how many fights can be won when you avoid conflict? What are some of the situations where you might need to stand and fight?

Play 'Call and Response' 12.1.1(a) as normal, except that whenever you call with a loud rumble, the group or individual you are working with must avoid your invitation to rumble and reply with a very soft rumble.

(F) PLAY HOW YOU FEEL

Ask participants to express any feelings they may have at the moment on their drum, emphasising that there is no right or wrong way to do this.

Remind participants of the need to constructively express feelings and that their drum can serve as a safe container in which to release their feelings.

(G) FEAR

Fear is something we all live with, but that can sometimes grow to the point where it becomes disabling, and we may spend our lives in avoidance, unable to move forward with our lives and fulfil our potential.

In this exercise we look at two different responses to fear and challenge people to move out of their comfort zone and face their fears, exploring the challenges and benefits of doing so and how we might extend this process to address other fears that are holding us hostage.

Start with a generalised conversation on fear - how it is a natural emotion that alerts us to danger, but can also become overwhelming and and leave us paralysed.

We might seek out examples of common fears, irrational fears, responses to fear and finish with examples or lessons from people who have faced up to, or overcome their fears.

The exercise starts with everyone playing a simple foundation rhythm and the facilitator showcasing a sharp pattern on a high pitched drum that is a warning of danger, like an alarm. On this signal group members are asked to freeze - no drumming, no movement or sound at all for an 8 count rest, before returning to the rhythm.

Practice and play this game a few times.

Then stop and point to the analogy between our fears and the way they stop us from moving forward.

The exercise starts over with the facilitator this time providing an additional option of facing up to our fears - "This time you can freeze or you can play through the silence, but if you play you need to make up your own rhythm & not play the foundation - in other words improvise.

Try this for a while so the rhythm flows with the solo break of 8 counts occurring regularly in-between.

Discuss who chose which course and why - how much did your self-belief influence your choice? How much was your decision influenced by the choices of those sitting next to you?

Finally place 3 chairs in the middle of the circle, in a tight triangle facing outward. This time we ask 3 people at a time to come into the middle and improvise together in the 8 bar gap. Rotate through the group so everyone gets a chance to be in the middle and share a few solos.

Finish with a discussion on how it felt to be in the middle and what this exercise might teach you in relation to facing your fears.

16.2 Additional Exercises for Communication

IND, GRP, FAM, COR. Age Range: 6 years and up.

(A) HAVE YOU EVER?

Ask the group a range of 'Have you ever…?' questions and get them to rumble if they have and stay silent if they haven't. Tell the group to ask one question each of the group but not to make it too personal.

(B) THE BEST DRUMMERS PLAY THE FEWEST NOTES

Pass out simple parts from one of the songs in the rhythm catalogue (Chapter 10) and before starting discuss this quote: 'The best drummers play the fewest notes.' Why would that be? Have you ever met someone who was careful with their words? What about people who never stop talking – how are they perceived? How easy is it for words to be misjudged?

Tell the participants you will raise your hand with one finger pointing into the air during this exercise and each time you do so they will remove one note from their rhythm, allowing more space into the overall sound (one finger raised = remove one note).

Start off the different rhythm parts and after a while gradually reduce the number of notes by raising your hand and pointing with one finger to the ceiling. Note the difference in clarity.

(C) COPY THAT

Start a pattern and send it round the room – each person should replicate what they get from the person next to them and send it on to the person on the farther side of them. Keep adding new rhythms – vary their complexity and note which are easier to communicate. Add a body movement to a rhythm and see if that is transferable as well. Depending on the size of the group, you may end up with several patterns rotating around the circle at the same time, which keeps everyone highly focused.

Utilise this exercise to explore a range of communication issues including the impact of rumour and cyber bullyng.

(D) TALK TO ME

Divide the group into pairs, who each have to come up with a two-part rhythmic phrase that talks and responds to each other (i.e. no overlapping). Try getting half of the whole group to play one half of this communication each and explore adding their own variations.

(E) DIALOGUE

Divide the group into pairs sitting across from each other in the circle and explain that each pair is to play a dialogue over the top of the group's rhythm. Have the group play a simple rhythm and showcase this with your co-facilitator or a chosen group member.

The two parts should talk to each other across the circle and still harmonise with the foundation rhythm. You can write up some simple dialogue parts on a white-board if your group members are finding it a challenge to make up their own (see parts from the exercise 'In Balance' 12.5.2(a)). Also remind them that they can take their time to find the right part and don't have to come in straight away – say that they should listen to their partner's part and adjust their part to 'speak' to his/hers. Give them a few minutes to practise this interlocking rhythmic dialogue.

Start a new foundation rhythm and one at a time introduce each pair – give them about two or three minutes each before moving on to the next pair.

Note: Lower the foundation volume each time a pair is playing.

(F) PLAY HOW YOU FEEL

Ask participants to express any feelings they may have at the moment on their drum, emphasising that there is no right or wrong way to do this.

Remind participants of the need to constructively express feelings and that their drum can serve as a safe container in which to release their feelings.

(G) FEAR

Fear is something we all live with, but that can sometimes grow to the point where it becomes disabling, and we may spend our lives in avoidance, unable to move forward with our lives and fulfil our potential.

In this exercise we look at two different responses to fear & challenge people to move out of their comfort zone and face their fears, exploring the challenges and benefits of doing so and how we might extend this process to address other fears that are holding us hostage.

Start with a generalised conversation on fear - how it is a natural emotion that alerts us to danger, but can also become overwhelming and and leave us paralysed.

We might seek out examples of common fears, irrational fears, responses to fear and finish with examples or lessons from people who have faced up to, or overcome their fears.

The exercise starts with everyone playing a simple foundation rhythm and the facilitator showcasing a sharp pattern on a high pitched drum that is a warning of danger, like an alarm. On this signal group members are asked to freeze - no drumming, no movement or sound at all for an 8 count rest, before returning to the rhythm.

Practice and play this game a few times.

Then stop and point to the analogy between our fears and the way they stop us from moving forward.

The exercise starts over with the facilitator this time providing an additional option of facing up to our fears - "This time you can freeze or you can play through the silence, but if you play you need to make up your own rhythm & not play the foundation - in other words improvise.

Try this for a while so the rhythm flows with the solo break of 8 counts occurring regularly in-between.

Discuss who chose which course and why - how much did your self-belief influence your choice? How much was your decision influenced by the choices of those sitting next to you?

Finally place 3 chairs in the middle of the circle, in a tight triangle facing outward. This time we ask 3 people at a time to come into the middle and improvise together in the 8 bar gap. Rotate through the group so everyone gets a chance to be in the middle and share a few solos.

Finish with a discussion on how it felt to be in the middle and what this exercise might teach you in relation to facing your fears.

16.3 Additional Exercises for Teamwork

IND, GRP, FAM, COR. Age Range: 6 years and up.

(A) THE TWO-WAY SHUFFLE
INSPIRED BY G. HUXTABLE, W. HUNN AND S. WITEK

Put people into pairs and then teach the following routine, breaking it down very slowly (people should sit opposite their partners with their drums touching). Both people count out an ongoing 1, 2, 3, 4 during the exercise and must start together. Choose who will be Person 1 (or A) and who will be Person 2 (or B).

Sequence 1

1. Person 1 (or A) – Two Tones on their own drum while Person 2 plays two pats on their legs (thighs).

    Person 2 (or B) – Two pats on their own legs while Person 1 plays two Tones (as above).

2. Person 1 – Two pats on their own legs while Person 2 plays two Tones on their own drum.

    Person 2 – Two Tones on their own drum while Person 1 plays two leg pats (as above).

Practise this until it is fluid.

Timing	1	+	2	+	3	+	4	+	1	+	2	+	3	+	4	+
1 or A	O		o		Thigh		Thigh		O		o		Thigh		Thigh	
2 or B	Thigh		Thigh		O		o		Thigh		Thigh		O		o	

Sequence 2

1. Person 1 – Two Tones on their own drum followed by two Tones on their *partner's* drum. That is each time both players are playing the same drum.

    Person 2 – Two Tones on their *partner's* drum followed by two Tones on their own drum.

Join the two sequences by agreeing on a signal for moving between the two, and speed up slowly.

Timing	1	+	2	+	3	+	4	+	1	+	2	+	3	+	4	+
1 or A	O		o		B's drum		B's drum		O		o		B's drum		B's drum	
2 or B	A's drum		A's drum		O		o		A's drum		A's drum		O		o	

Advanced

1. Person 1 – Two Tones (own drum) followed by two pats on their legs.

    Person 2 – Two pats on their legs followed by two Tones on their own drum.

2. Person 1 – Two Tones on partner's drum followed by two pats on their legs.

    Person 2 – Two pats on their legs followed by two Tones on their partner's drum.

Start slowly and speed up.

Timing	1	+	2	+	3	+	4	+	1	+	2	+	3	+	4	+
1 or A	O		o		Thigh		Thigh		B's drum		B's drum		Thigh		Thigh	
2 or B	Thigh		Thigh		O		o		Thigh		Thigh		A's drum		A's drum	

(B) PASS IT

In this exercise you pass one note or a series of notes from one person to another in a specific sequence. First agree upon the order for passing – you can use birthdays, oldest to youngest or the alphabetical order of their names.

Play one note only each and ask the group to pass that note evenly around the circle in the agreed order. The group members have to remember the order and then work on how quickly they can get that rhythm moving – one participant can time it on a stopwatch.

Other options include:

• trying it with different percussion

• trying it with eyes closed

• trying it with the tone chimes, but the time element reversed – how slowly can we send it?

16.4 Generic Exercises

IND, GRP, FAM, COR. Age Range: 8 years and up.

(A) LAYERING IN, ONE PERSON AT A TIME

One person starts a simple rhythm, and one at a time each person enters the rhythm with a beat of their own choice. Each individual can enter after the person next to them or alternatively diagonally across the circle. Once the whole group is playing, the facilitator can use a range of facilitation techniques to add different dynamics to the group rhythm.

Discuss the challenges of connection, communication, harmony and teamwork using this exercise. How important was having a stable platform to add to? What might that platform represent?

(B) MAKE UP YOUR OWN

Whenever people are playing set patterns, it can be empowering to offer them the opportunity to segue into playing their own rhythm, by adjusting what they are playing to 'make it your own'. This can be challenging for some people who appreciate the safety of a set patterns, but in time can help foster the creativity, flexibility and self-belief necessary for adaption to changing life circumstances.

(C) MAKE UP YOUR OWN – SOLO

The participants play a simple 4/4 foundation rhythm and use a signal to stop (4, 3, 2, 1, STOP on the first note of the next bar) and then rest for seven counts before resuming play – practise this until it is tight.

Then have each person spend five minutes working out a simple solo phrase they can play in that seven-count gap – showcase a few examples to help those who are less confident and offer the opportunity to add voice or additional percussion instruments if available.

Examine how self-confidence and support influence creativity and problem solving.

(D) MUSICAL CHAIRS VERSION 2
A REGULATION EXERCISE

Issues Addressed: Focus, listening, regulation, change, perspective.

Showcase two similar signals on a bell:

1. Three clear strikes of the bell.

2. Two clear strikes, a gap and then another strike.

Play musical chairs and practise using one of the different patterns each time the rhythm stops for the seven rest.

Then explain that only number one bell pattern means move from your seat, while number two means stop and stay in your chair.

See how well people can recognise the difference and respond correctly – moving seats on number one bell call and staying in the same place if you use number two.

Discuss how challenging it was to recognise the difference and respond correctly.

Note: Use more challenging signals if these are too easy (e.g. different melodies on the bell).

16.5 Exercises for Numeracy and Literacy

IND, GRP. Age Range: 5 years and up.

(A) STRIKE OUT
As a group, agree upon a number between three and nine.

Start off a count from one upwards around the circle – each time a number that includes your chosen number is mentioned, you must hit your drum instead of saying that number.

Advanced
Additionally add any number that is divisible by the agreed upon number.

(B) HOW MANY BEATS?

Play a certain number of strikes on your instrument and ask participants to count how many there are each time you play. Extend this to include addition and multiplication (e.g. three times a set of three beats equals nine beats).

(C) COUNTING ON YOU

Use the 'Counting on You' 12.5.2(b) exercise.

(D) READING IN RHYTHM

Have people read a sentence each while playing a steady rhythm – pace the rhythm to their developmental reading speed and see if it assists their fluidity.

17

REFLECTIVE PRACTICE AND EVALUATIVE RESOURCES

The question 'How do you know what you are doing is working?' has become an essential ethical consideration for the modern-day practitioner. Sadly, for many people presenting for therapy or psycho-social education today, that question receives only minor consideration. The presumption that a trained professional will know how to help, backed by the huge political power exercised by professional organisations, academic institutions and drug companies, makes questioning this belief tantamount to insurrection. Yet professionals in the therapy field, as well as many researchers, have long been questioning the over-prescribing of drugs (particularly anti-depressants), the limits of cognitive-based therapies and the efficacy of a number of other well-established health practices (Holmes, 2002; Seligman, 2011).

Meta analysis research into the efficacy of therapeutic interventions has shown that a number of our professional assumptions are wrong: evidence-based practice is not an indicator of client outcomes, nor is any specific technique or model (Imel *et al.,* 2008). Neither academic qualifications nor membership of professional associations have a positive impact on a client's level of recovery. What is known to really make a difference is the quality of the therapeutic relationship and the degree of client-informed, reflective practice that the practitioner engages in (Miller *et al.,* 2004). These two elements above all others influence client outcomes, and as such must be given priority in our practice.

We have discussed previously the way that rhythmic music can facilitate improved connection between a practitioner and those they work with, reducing the shame and resistance that is often associated with talk-based therapies. Client-informed, reflective practice is the other half of the 'effective practice' formula and involves regularly consulting those we support on their perceived progress towards the mutually conceived goals agreed upon at the beginning of our work together. These consultations can take the form of interviews or questionnaires (see the downloadable materials) and are most effective when connected to statistical markers that represent progress to, or from, the goals of the intervention.

This form of evaluation is client centred, and empowering, and the feedback is then incorporated into the way the practitioner works with the client into the future. Key areas of feedback include a person's treatment preferences, including the focus areas of the intervention, its duration and intensity and who will deliver it. In school-based psycho-social education, this form of client-centred evaluation will need to be tempered by the logistical imperatives of a school system, but in saying that, there are still many options for the practitioner to tailor the delivery of a Rhythm2Recovery intervention in line with the feedback of participants. Simple questionnaires that canvas likes and dislikes with regard to different elements of the model and its delivery, and questions that explore participant motivation and goal orientation, can help ensure a program will be better directed and more strategic in the way it goes about supporting its participants and achieving its purpose.

The following is a list of appropriate questionnaires and other validated measures that can be useful in evaluating a Rhythm2Recovery intervention. It is important that practitioners utilise these tests in accordance with ethical standards and only use tests for which they are suitably qualified and trained. All tests have a cultural bias and results must be considered in light of this.

- Working Alliance Inventory Client (WAIC) Therapist (WAIT). Examines the collaborative relationship between helper and the client, meaning that there is a consensus and willingness on the part of both parties to engage in and do the work that leads to improvement. Available at: http://wai.profhorvath.com/downloads, accessed 15 May 2016.

- Group Climate Questionnaire (GCQ). The GCQ consists of 12 items, which assess members' perceptions of the group's therapeutic environment including engagement, avoidance and conflict. Available at: www.oqmeasures.com/measures/group-measures/gcq-s, accessed 15 May 2016.

- Outcome Rating Scale (ORS). The ORS consists of four items that assess how clients are doing within social, inter-personal and individual domains. Available at: http://scott-d-miller-ph-d.myshopify.com/collections/performance-metrics/products, accessed 15 May 2016.

- Strengths and Difficulties Questionnaires (SDQ). A range of questionnaires designed to assess social and emotional issues that impact behaviour for 3–16-year-olds, which is utilised by a wide range of organisations working with young people. Different questionnaires are provided to obtain perspectives from both the young person and an observing adult. Available at: www.sdqinfo.com, accessed 15 May 2016.

- Behavioural and Emotional Rating Scale (BERS-2). Examines a young person's (5–18 years) inter-personal strengths, functioning in and at school, affective strength, intra-personal strength, family involvement and career strength. Designed to be used in school settings, mental health clinics, juvenile justice settings and child welfare agencies. Available at: www.proedinc.com/customer, accessed 15 May 2016.

- Social Skills Improvement System (SSIS) Rating Scales. This test offers a targeted and comprehensive assessment of a young person's (3–18 years) social skills, problem behaviours and academic competence. Available at: www.pearsonclinical.com, accessed 15 May 2016.

- Kessler Psychological Distress Scale (K10). This is a ten-item questionnaire intended to yield a global measure of distress based on questions about anxiety and depressive symptoms that a person has experienced in the most recent four-week period. Available at: www.hcp.med.harvard.edu/ncs/k6_scales.php, accessed 15 May 2016.

- Becks Depression Inventory (BDI). A 21-question, multiple-choice, self-report inventory for individuals aged 13 years and over. One of the most widely used psychometric tests for measuring the severity of depression. Available at: www.pearsonclinical.com, accessed 15 May 2016.

- Rosenberg's Self-Esteem Scale (SES). The most widely used self-esteem scale. A ten-item scale that measures global self-worth by measuring both positive and negative feelings about the self. The scale is believed to be uni-dimensional. Available at: www.wwnorton.com/college/psych/psychsci/media/rosenberg.htm, accessed 15 May 2016.

See the downloadable materials for additional questionnaires.

FURTHER READING

Currie, M. (2008) *Doing Anger Differently*. Melbourne: University Press.

DePree, M. (2008) *Leadership Jazz*. Sydney: Doubleday.

Faulkner, S. (2006) *The Drum as a Healing Tool in Therapeutic Practice*. Victoria Park WA: Holyoake Institute. Available at: http://holyoake.org.au, accessed 15 May 2016.

Friedman, R. L. (2011) *The Healing Power of the Drum, Book 2*. Gilsum, NH: White-Cliffs Media.

Hanko, J. (2011) *100 Learning Games for Special Needs With Music, Movement, Sounds and…Silence*. London: Jessica Kingsley Publishers.

Harris, R. (2009) *ACT Made Simple*. Oakland, CA: New Harbinger Publications.

Holland, D. (2007) *Drumimagination*. Self-published. Available at: http://interactiverhythm.com, accessed 15 May 2016.

Holland, D. (2015) *Body Jammin*. Self-published. Available at: http://interactiverhythm.com, accessed 15 May 2016.

Hull, A. (2006) *Drum Circle Facilitation: Building Community Through Rhythm*. Santa Cruz, CA: Village Music Circles.

Hull, A. (2013) *Rhythmical Alchemy Playshop: Volume 1 – Drum-Circle Games*. Santa Cruz, CA: Village Music Circles.

Kynsh, M. (2013) *Innovative Drum-Circles: Beyond Beat Into Harmony*. PA: Rhythmic Connections Publications.

Kynsh, M. and Leathley, L. (2015) *1, 2, Let's All Play*. PA: Rhythmic Connections Publications.

Levitin, D. J. (2006) *This Is Your Brain on Music*. London: Atlantic Books.

Levitin, D. J. (2008) *The World in Six Songs*: New York, NY: Dutton/Penguin.

MacTavish, H. and Balsara, Z. (2012) *Songs, Science, Spirit: Musical Keys to Open Special Doors of Ability*. CA: Provident Publishing.

Masala, K. S. (2004) *Rhythm Play*. Austin, TX: Kenya Masala and Source Consulting Group.

Oshinsky, J. *Return to Child: Music for People's Guide to Improvised Music and Authentic Group Leadership*. Available at: http://musicforpeople.org/wp, accessed 15 May 2016.

Sacks, O. (2007) *Musicophilia*. New York, NY: Random House.

Schneck, D. J. and Berger, D. S. (2006) *The Music Effect. Music Psychology and Clinical Applications*. Philadelphia, PA: Jessica Kingsley Publishers.

Seligman, M. (2011) *Flourish*. Sydney: Random House.

Small, C. (1977). *Education, Music Society*. Middletown Connecticut: Wesleyan University Press.

Stevens, C. (2003) *The Art and Heart of Drum Circles*. Milwaukee, WI: Hal Leonard.

SIMON'S BIO

If you want to know a little bit about my past and how it connects to this work, well, read on.

For much of my working life I was a gardener. I ran my own nursery, growing plants for sale, had a display garden for garden enthusiasts to visit and designed and installed gardens for other people. I consider my work as a counsellor an extension of this same passion: nurturing the best out of people and providing the right conditions to optimise growth. My grandparents were educators who stirred my passion for gardening, and in the early 20th century they established a 'radical' school experiment that married education to the running of an agricultural farm in northern Tasmania (Australia). They strongly believed that practical, experiential education was a powerful model for academic, social and personal development and their students spent many hours in food production, much of which ended up on their plates in the dining room each evening.

When I had my own children I was living in rural Western Australia, and I became involved in youth work, initially as a volunteer, and later, after returning to tertiary education, as a new career. I spent a lot of my early years in the youth sector, working with the consequences of drugs and alcohol and completed a double major in psychology and addiction. It was doing preventative drug and alcohol psycho-education that led me to the experience, described in the introduction of this manual, which brought rhythmic music into my practice.

In 2003 I developed the Holyoake DRUMBEAT program, which became a well-established social and emotional learning program in schools across Australia and was utilised for other populations experiencing social and emotional challenges. I was fortunate to receive a Churchill Fellowship in 2005 and travelled across North America researching the use of rhythm-based interventions in health and educational settings, including observing traditional methods employed by First Nations people.

My work has taken me into a wide range of environments and allowed me to work with, and learn from, people of all ages and from a wide range of backgrounds in many different countries. In all those situations I have found people with a natural affinity for rhythmic music and the subtle lessons it can impart. Adaptations of the DRUMBEAT program were developed for people with 'complex needs' and for parents, and the research base of the program grew, with several independent studies supporting its efficacy as a mental health intervention. I also worked with a computer game developer to design an interactive therapeutic computer game called 'DRUMBEAT Quest', which is played on a drum console and is aligned to the Australian Health Curriculum.

I left my work with DRUMBEAT behind after 12 years and started expanding the Rhythm2Recovery model to incorporate the growing evidence supporting the newer, third-wave, behavioural therapies, as well as the neurological research into the impact of rhythmic music on the brain, particularly in relation to trauma. My practice has expanded from the youth, drug and alcohol, and mental health fields to include work with prisoners, aged care residents, veterans and most recently the corporate sector, where problem behaviours and dysfunctional relationship are equally costly.

I remain a keen gardener and am always appreciative of rain.

REFERENCES

Austin, D. (2001) 'In search of the self: The use of vocal holding techniques with adults traumatized as children.' *Music Therapy Perspectives 19*, 1, 22–30.

Austin, D. (2008) *The Theory and Practice of Vocal Psychotherapy*. London: Jessica Kingsley Publishers.

Australian Institute of Health and Welfare (2013) *Depression in Residential Aged Care 2008–2012*. Aged Care Statistics Series No. 39. Cat. no. AGE 73. Canberra: Australian Institute of Health and Welfare.

Bennett, M.P. and Lengacher, C. (2008). 'Humour and laughter may influence health. III. Laughter and health outcomes.' *Evidence Based Complementary Alternative Medicine 5*, 1, 37–40.

Bensimon, M., Amir, D. and Wolf, Y. (2008) 'Drumming through trauma: Music therapy with post-traumatic soldiers.' *The Arts in Psychotherapy, 35*, 34–48.

Biggs, J. (2001). *Enhancing Learning: A Matter of Style or Approach? Perspectives on Thinking, Learning and Cognitive Styles*, R. J. Sternberg, L. F. Zhang (eds.). Mahwah, Lawrance Erlbaum Associates, N. J.

Blenkiron, P. (2011) *Stories and Analogies in Cognitive Behaviour Therapy*. Chichester: John Wiley and Sons.

Bernardi, L., Sleight, P., Bandinelli, G., Cencetti, S. *et al.* (2001) 'Effect of rosary prayer and yoga mantras on autonomic cardiovascular rhythms: Comparative study.' *British Medical Journal, 323*, 22–29.

Brinol, P. and Petty, R. E. (2008) 'Embodied Persuasion: Fundamental Processes by Which Bodily Responses Can Impact Attitudes.' In G. R. Semin and E. R. Smith (eds) *Embodiment Grounding: Social, Cognitive, Affective, and Neuroscientific Approaches*. Cambridge: Cambridge University Press.

Campitelli, G. and Gobet, F. (2011) 'Deliberate practice necessary, but not sufficient.' *Current Directions in Psychological Science 20*, 5, 280–285.

Carr, E. G., Dunlap, G., Horner, R. H., Koegel, R. L. *et al.* (2002). 'Positive behavior support: Evolution of an applied science.' *Journal of Positive Behavior Interventions 4*, 4–6.

Chanda L. C. and Levitin, D. J. (2013) 'The neurochemistry of music.' *Trends in Cognitive Sciences 17*, 4. 179–193.

Chatto, A. (1996) *Brief History of Drumming*. Canadian Associates Drumming Rudimental Excellence. Available at: http://cadre-online.ca/brief-history-of-drumming, accessed on 10 May 2016.

Clift, S., Hancox, G., Staricoff, R. and Whitmore, C. (2008) *Singing and Health: A Systematic Mapping and Review of Non-Clinical Research*. Canterbury: Canterbury Christ Church University.

Csikszentmihalyi, M. (1997). *Finding Flow: The Psychology of Engagement With Everyday Life*. New York, NY: Basic Books.

DeCasper, A. J., Lacaneut, J., Busnel, M., Granier-Defer, C. and Maugeais, R. (1994) 'Foetal reactions to recurrent maternal speech.' *Infant Behaviour and Development 17*, 159–164.

Duncan, B. L., and Miller, S.D. (2004). *The Heroic Client: Principles of Client Directed, Outcome-Informed Therapy* (revised edition). San Francisco, CA: Jossey- Bass.

Durlak, J. A., Weissberg, R. P., Dymnicki, A. B., Taylor, R. D. and Schellinger, K. B. (2011) 'The impact of enhancing students' social and emotional learning: A meta-analysis of school-based universal interventions.' *Child Development 82*, 1, 405–432.

Eckersly, R. (2006) 'Is modern Western culture a health hazard?' *International Journal of Epidemiology 35*, 2, 252–258.

Emmons, G. P. and McKendryAnderson, L. M. (2005) *Understanding Sensory Dysfunction*. London: Jessica Kingsley Publishers.

Fancourt, D., Perkins, R., Ascenso, S., Carvalho, L. A., Steptoe, A. and Williamon, A. (2016) 'Effects of group drumming interventions on anxiety, depression, social resilience and inflammatory immune response among mental health service users.' PLOS ONE *11*, 3 e0151136. doi:10.1371/journal.pone.0151136.

Flores, K. (2011) *African drumming as a medium to promote emotional and social well-being of children aged 7 to 12 in residential care.* Thesis, Doctorate of Music, University of Pretoria Faculty of Humanities Department of Music. Available at: http://repository.up.ac.za/bitstream/handle/2263/25630/Complete.pdf?sequence=5, accessed on 10 May 2016.

Friedman, R. L. (2000) *The Healing Power of the Drum.* Reno, NV: White Cliffs Media.

Garcia Coll, C. and Marks, A. K. (2009) *Immigrant Stories: Ethnicity and Academics in Middle Childhood.* New York, NY: Oxford University Press.

Hari, J. (2015) *Chasing the Scream: The First and Last Days on the War on Drugs.* New York, NY: Bloomsbury.

Hayes, S. C., Strosahl, K. and Wilson, K. G. (1999). *Acceptance and Commitment Therapy: An Experiential Approach to Behaviour Change.* New York, NY: Guilford Press.

Holmes, J. (2002) 'All you need is cognitive behavioural therapy?' *British Journal of Medicine, 324,* 288–294.

Holyoake Institute (2009) *The DRUMBEAT Program: A Review of Three Formative Programs in Mental Health Settings.* Internal Report. Victoria Park WA: Holyoake Institute. Available at: www.holyoake.org.au/files//DRUMBEAT/DRUMBEAT%20in%20Mental%20Health%20settings.pdf, accessed on 10 May 2016.

Imel, Z. E., Wampold, B. E., Miller, S. D. and Fleming, R. R. (2008) 'Distinctions without a difference: Direct comparisons of psychotherapists for alcohol use disorders.' *Journal of Addictive Behaviours,* 533–543.

Kenyon G. P. and Thaut M. H. (2000) 'A measure of kinematic limb instability modulation by rhythmic auditory stimulation.' *Journal of Biomechanics 33,* 1319–1323.

Kilroy, D. (2001) *When will they see the real us? Women in prisons.* Paper presented at the Women in Corrections: Staff and Individuals Conference, Adelaide. 31 October–1 November 2000. Available at: www.sistersinside.com.au/media/whenwillyouseetherealus.pdf, accessed on 10 May 2016.

Kounin, J. (1971) *Discipline and Group Management in Classrooms.* New York, NY: Holt, Rinehart, and Winston.

Levitin, D. J. (2009) *The World in Six Songs: How the Musical Brain Created Human Nature.* London: Penguin.

Lou, C. (2008) *The Transformative Power of Metaphor in Therapy.* New York, NY: Springer Publishing.

Mabbott, D. J., Noseworthy, M., Bouffet, E., Laughlin, S. and Rockel C. (2006) 'White matter growth as a mechanism of cognitive development in children.' *Neuroimage 33,* 936–946.

MacTavish, H. (2012) *Songs, Science and Spirit: Musical Keys to Open Special Doors Of Ability.* Cotati, CA: Provident Publishing.

McGarry, L. M. and Russo, F. A. (2011) 'Mirroring in dance/movement therapy: Potential mechanisms behind empathy enhancement.' *The Arts in Psychotherapy 38,* 178–184.

Medina, J. (2008) *Brain Rules: 12 Principles for Surviving and Thriving at Work.* Seattle, WA: Pear Press.

Miller, S. (2010) *What works in therapy.* Presentation at Australian AOD conference, Fremantle, WA (23-25 June 2014). Available at: http://scottdmiller.com/wp-content/uploads/What%20Works%202010.PDF, accessed on 10 May 2016.

Miller, S. D., Meel Lee, D., Plum, B. and Hubble, M. A. (2005) 'Making treatment count.' *Psychotherapy in Australia 11,* 4, 42–56.

Norcross, J. (2009) 'The Therapeutic Relationship.' In B. Duncan, S. Miller, B. Wampold and M. Hubble (eds) *The Heart and Soul of Change.* Washington, DC: APA Press.

Ogden, P., Minton, K. and Pain, C. (2006) *Trauma and the Body: A Sensorimotor Approach to Psychotherapy.* New York, NY: Norton.

Perry, B. D. and Hambrick, E. (2008) 'Introduction to the neurosequential model of therapeutics.' *Reclaiming Youth, 17, 3,* 38–43.

Pollard, J. A., Hawkins, J. D. and Arthur, M. W. (1999) 'Risk and protection: Are both necessary to understand diverse behavioural outcomes in adolescence.' *Social Work Research 23, 3,* 145–158.

Read, N. (2006). *Sick and Tired: Healing the Illnesses That Doctors Cannot Cure.* UK: London Phoenix.

Rice, N., and Follette, V. M. (2003) 'The Termination and Referral of Clients.' In: W. O'Donohue, and K. Ferguson (eds) *Handbook of Professional Ethics for Psychologists: Issues, Questions, and Controversies.* Thousand Oaks, CA: SAGE Publications.

Richardson, L. K., Frueh, B. C. and Acierno, R. (2010) 'Prevalence estimates of combat-related PTSD: A critical review.' *Australian and New Zealand Journal of Psychiatry 44, 1,* 4–19.

Sacks, O. (2007). *Musicophilia: Tales of Music and the Brain.* New York, NY: Random House.

Schneck, D. J. and Berger, D. S. (2005) *The Music Effect: Music Psychology and Clinical Application.* New York, NY: Jessica Kingsley Publishers.

Seligman, M. (2011) *Flourish.* New York, NY: Free Press.

Slotoroff, C. (1994) 'Drumming technique for assertiveness and anger management in the short-term psychiatric setting for adult and adolescent survivors of trauma.' *Music Therapy Perspectives 12, 2,* 111–116.

Strong, J. (2015) *Different Drummer: One Man's Music and Its Impact on ADD, Anxiety, and Autism.* Santa Fe, NM: Strong Institute.

Sumari, M. and Jalal, F. H. (2008) 'Cultural issues in counseling: An international perspective.' *Counselling, Psychotherapy, and Health 4, 1,* 24–34.

Tamplin, J. (2008) 'A pilot study into the effect of vocal exercises and singing on dysarthric speech.' *NeuroRehabilitation 23, 3,* 207–2016.

Thaut M. H., Kenyon G. P., Schauer M. L. and McIntosh G. C. (1999) 'The connection between rhythmicity and brain function: Implications for therapy of movement disorders.' *Engineering in Medicine and Biology Magazine 18,* 101–108.

Van Der Kolk, B. (2014) *The Body Keeps the Score.* New York: Allen Lane.

Winkleman, M. (2003) 'Complementary therapy for addiction: Drumming out drugs.' *American Journal of Public Health 93, 4,* 647–651.

Wolvin, A. D. and Coakley, C. G. (1995) *Listening.* New York, NY: McGraw Hill Education.

Yoon, J. S. (2002) 'Teacher characteristics as predictors of teacher–student relationships: Stress, negative-affect and self-efficacy.' *Social Behaviour and Personality 30,* 485–493.

Zillman, D. and Gan. S. (1997) 'Musical Tastes in Adolescence.' In D. J.Hargraves, and A. C. North *The Social Psychology of Music.* Oxford: Oxford University Press.

SUBJECT INDEX

AUTHOR INDEX